Zohar

The Ultimate Guide to Understanding the Most Important Work on Kabbalah and Jewish Mysticism

Your Free Gift (only available for a limited time)

Thanks for getting this book! If you want to learn more about various spirituality topics, then join Mari Silva's community and get a free guided meditation MP3 for awakening your third eye. This guided meditation mp3 is designed to open and strengthen ones third eye so you can experience a higher state of consciousness. Simply visit the link below the image to get started.

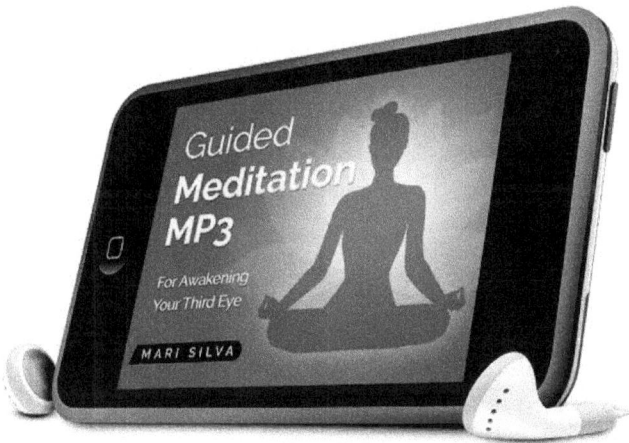

https://spiritualityspot.com/meditation

Contents

Introduction

The Zohar is the primary sacred text of Kabbalah and has allegorical and mystical representations and interpretations of various Jewish sacred books, including the Torah. The Zohar and the wisdom of Kabbalah are emerging from the depths of history to help us move forward to higher spiritual dimensions. It is interesting to discover why the ancient wisdom of Kabbalah is gaining prominence in modern times.

The growth and development of humankind have been in a state of flux. Our needs were simple and basic in ancient times - food, clothing, shelter, and procreation. As humankind developed, so did our needs and desires, which progressed from basic to advanced such as wealth, power, domination, and knowledge.

Right through history, we have been working on satisfying our needs. We changed our lifestyle and habits as our needs changed. We chased and even achieved our materialistic dreams in the hope that when realized, we would be happy. In the modern world, the ubiquitous media continues to tempt us to more and more with materialistic choices, and we embrace these temptations to feel satisfied and complete.

Each time we get a better-paying job, a new car, a bigger home, a bigger title, or any such thing, for a while, we are happy. But the inner emptiness returns. Humans have realized that the chase for materialism is futile and that our happiness is not based on how much wealth, power, or domination we have.

We have seen that, especially in recent times, the more "advanced" we become, the more we suffer. We even find happiness has driven a few of us to drugs, antidepressants, and alcohol, in the hope that we can fill our internal emptiness. We ask ourselves, "How much longer is this chase for eternal happiness? When and where will I find it?"

Nowhere before in the history of humankind have such deep questions for harmony and peace been so powerful and prevalent as they are today. In ancient times, only the "highly learned" and esoteric scholars asked these questions. They found the answers too, but kept them hidden for the right time.

Today, even the average common man is riddled with these deep questions? We have truly realized the worthlessness of materialism and know that it can never give us the true happiness we seek. The time is ripe for the ancient wisdom of Kabbalah to surface and help people find what they truly seek.

There is another interesting reason for the wisdom of Kabbalah to find relevance in today's technologically advanced world. Thanks to the internet and its ability to connect humans even from remote corners of the world, we live in a global village. Yet, our over-inflated egos and high intolerance levels toward each other obstruct the path to authentic interdependence and a life of harmony.

We have become wealthy enough to build large homes so that each of us has a separate room for ourselves. We have built walls around us in the name of privacy. Sadly, we have also built walls around our hearts. We find it exceedingly difficult to maintain relationships, and families are falling apart.

We live in a cramped environment thanks to the booming world population, yet we remain intolerant of each other. The strength of advanced weapons we have control over has made this world a highly unstable and dangerous place. Despite the immense growth and development of human civilization, we seem to have remained in the man-eat-man world of our hunter-gatherer ancestor world.

If we continue to do this, how will we survive? Even if we survive, what kind of world will we be leaving for our children? It is interesting to note that the present generation is perhaps the first to know and accept that their world was better than the world their children live in. That is to say, we have finally accepted that our world is devolving instead of evolving, despite all the technological "progress" we have made.

This search for the elusive sense of peace and true happiness has led people to Kabbalah and the Zohar. Although the subject is deep and full of esotericism, if someone were to ask you what Zohar is, you could answer with this simple definition. "*The Zohar explains the authentic way of life you can follow in today's stressful times based on ancient wisdom left behind by wise people who predicted that such times would come.*"

A similar situation happened in ancient Babylon thousands of years ago. The story of the Tower of Babel described in the Bible talks about how people gathered in one place to discuss how to build a gigantic tower that would touch the sky. Metaphorically, this tower represents the indefatigable ego of humans. The gathering of people represented their interdependence, which did not reduce the hatred among them. The wisdom of Kabbalah appeared at that point in time.

The Kabbalists believe that Abraham, the Patriarch, who lived in Ur, Chaldeans, realized that humankind's progress was moving toward finding a reality based on materialism, quite different from what was intended for humans. Abraham realized that eventually, the energy toward finding a material world would exhaust itself at some point in time, and we will realize that we need something beyond corporeal elements to live a meaningful and fulfilling life.

Abraham realized that spiritual evolution would begin when material evolution ends. Once we achieve many of our materialistic desires and realize that we are still not happy, we begin searching for our life's real purpose. In Kabbalah, "the heart" represents earthly desires, and "the point in the heart" is the desire to discover the true meaning of life.

That point in the heart awakens the heart and drives us to spiritual evolution. When Abraham connected with "the point in his heart," he discovered the authentic reality or spiritual wisdom, and this wisdom realized by Abraham is called the "wisdom of Kabbalah."

The wisdom of Kabbalah is simple and easy to understand. At its core, Kabbalah says that over and above the reality that humans sense with our five senses, there is a much larger, higher, and more expansive reality. The forces in this higher reality govern the reality as experienced by humans.

Thousands of years of development of the human world were intended to help us recognize this higher reality that governs us, and we will realize this truth when we recognize the higher reality. And when this happens, we can break through the confines of our human lives and know life in its everlasting, eternal form.

Today, Kabbalism is known as the mystical and esoteric tradition of Judaism. However, Kabbalah is an ancient spiritual heritage that predates Judaism. It also goes beyond the identification of any nation, ethnicity, or religion. Kabbalah is a large body of spiritual teachings and wisdom and should not be relegated to any single "religion." Kabbalists believe that Kabbalah should not be termed as "religious" at all, considering the teachings in this belief system are not based on blind obedience to laws or commandments.

Kabbalah is not limited to literal interpretations of scriptures and sacred texts. Followers are not frightened into observing the laws through fear of punishment. Also, Kabbalah does not talk about the need to "transcend" anything to achieve divine wisdom or the "ecstatic" achievement of reaching the "divine."

On the contrary, logical analysis of spiritual matters is a critical aspect of Kabbalism. The book you are reading attempts to tell you what the Zohar and Kabbalah are all about. You will learn how you can use the teachings of the Zohar in your life and transform yourself positively.

Many interesting questions about the Zohar are answered in this book, including who wrote it and its origins. The Zohar is centered upon Rabbi Shimon (or Rabbi Simeon) and his companions, and the text itself names him as the author.

Modern scholars argue that Moses de Leon of Spain wrote a large part of the book in the 13th century A.D. They also agree that the Spanish author is likely to have used and incorporated multiple mystical and spiritual resources from the earlier times to compile the Zohar.

The mysterious nature of creation is a recurring theme in it. It also discusses the cosmic significance of doing good deeds and prayers and the problem of evil. To understand the importance of the Zohar in Kabbalah, it may make more sense to note here that Kabbalists accord it the same reverence as they do to the Talmud and Torah.

There is little doubt that the questions addressed and the book's answers are complex and often confusing. Yet there is also little doubt that believers and scholars revere the Zohar as one of the most wondrous works on esoteric thought. It may take a little longer to understand the deep meanings it conveys. But when you persist in your effort, you will be sufficiently rewarded with clarity of thought and lessons that help you take your life up a few notches in your spiritual journey.

That explains what the Zohar contains. Read on to discover more about this wondrous book and its contents.

Chapter One: The Context of the Zohar

The Zohar or the Sefer ha-Zohar or the "Book of Splendor" is considered the most important sacred text of Jewish mysticism. The Jews render it the same importance as they do on the Talmud and the Old Testament.

And yet, we must reiterate what was said in the introduction chapter. Kabbalah cannot be relegated to any single religion or philosophy consisting of unquestionable tenets. Instead, it is best to think of Kabbalah as a collection of analytical tools, guidebooks, practical applications, and a few oracles instead of seeing it as an academic philosophy or one religion.

When we see something as a practical tool, then the chances of using it in our daily lives are higher. We tend to see how these ideas and concepts can be made practical and how to put them to use in our lives. This approach also helps us see Kabbalah as belonging to everyone and not merely be seen as esoteric verses or words that can be understood only by the original authors or those who have spent many years studying it.

The Zohar is the central sacred text of Kabbalah. It is believed to be the ultimate book on the wisdom of Kabbalah. Before you read on, the first thing you must do is discard or unlearn conventional religious expectations from the teachings in the Zohra. You can grasp the kabbalistic principles in the Zohar when your mind is free not only of conventional religious ideas but also mechanical, linear scientific, and rational thoughts. The Zohar goes beyond all religions and sciences, including all the technological advancements of the modern world.

What does the Zohar actually contain? It is a commentary on the Torah or the Five Books of Moses, which is also called the first five books of the Bible. It also explains the meaning of texts in the Book of Ruth and the Song of Solomon. The Zohar has lengthy homilies interspersed appropriately with parables and short discourses.

The Zohar has many layers. At one level, the hero in the Zohar is Rabbi Shimon, who lived in Israel in the second century. He was the son of Yohai, a saint. Rabbi Shimon and his companions discovered and shared the secrets of the Torah as they wandered around the hills of Galilee.

At another level, the biblical characters Abraham and Sarah become the primary protagonists while Rabbi Shimon and his companions interpret their behaviors, actions, and thoughts. At a much deeper level, the Bible is only a starting point that students and learners can use as a springboard for their imagination. Here is a classic example to explain this deep level of the Zohar.

In the Bible, God commands Abraham as follows, "Lekh lekha!" The usual translation of this would be, "Go to the land that I will show you." However, the Zohar emphasizes reading the message from God literally, which means "Go to yourself." So, on a deeper level, God commands Abraham to delve deep into his own being and find the divine hidden within.

At other times, Rabbi Shimon's companions become the main characters. This happens when we read about their mystical sessions with Rabbi Shimon in which they undergo multiple adventures, each of which has a deeper meaning and lesson to be learned. An example of such an approach in the Zohar goes as follows. The companions, while traveling with Rabbi Shimon, encounter an old, cantankerous donkey driver. Soon, they discover this man was a wise sage in disguise.

The ultimate aim of the Zohar is to focus on the ten "sefirot." This concept is discussed in detail in the final section of this book. Yet, it makes sense to introduce it here in brief. The etymology of "sefirot" is rooted in a word that means "to count." It represents various stages of God's life, including His divine personality, including feminine and masculine aspects.

Who Wrote the Zohar?

The previous chapter explained that the Zohra was written by Moses de Leon, a Spaniard, in the 13th century A.D. However, the text itself names Rabbi Shimon or Simeon ben Yohai, who lived in the 2nd century, as the author. Let us look at these two people in a bit of detail.

Simeon ben Yohai - Simeon ben Yohai was a scholar who lived and flourished in the 2nd century. He was a Galilean Tanna, a select and prestigious group of Palestinian rabbinic teachers and scholars. He was one of the most eminent and famous disciples of Rabbi Akiba ben Joseph. Traditionally, he is considered to be the author of the Zohar. Multiple legends have sprouted around this man, many of which are described in the Talmud.

During Roman rule, it was difficult for Kabbalists and followers of Judaism in the Land of Israel to live and follow their faith in peace. There was rampant persecution of Jews, and studying the Torah, Talmud, or any other sacred texts of Judaism was banned. If any, when one was found learning the Talmud or Torah, death was the only punishment.

In these daunting times, Rabbi Simeon was ordained to study the Torah along with four other rabbis by Rabbi Akiva. The persecutors went after the five ordained scholars. Although they managed to escape, Rabbi Akiva was captured and sentenced to death, and he became a martyr to the Jewish cause.

After the revered rabbi's death, Simeon and other pupils of Akiva's academy, including the saintly Rabbi Meir, opposed the Romans. He was forced to flee and hide himself to escape death by the Romans. Rabbi Simeon went into hiding with his son, Rabbi Elazar. At first, they hid at Rabbi Akiva's Academy, where Rabbi Simeon's wife brought them food and water every day. But, when the search intensified, the father and son found a better hiding place, telling no one so the rest of the family could maintain their ignorance and remain safe.

Legends say that Simeon and his son, Elazar, hid in a cave for 13 years, eating only a carob tree's pods and dates. When they came out of hiding, Simeon opened an academy and taught many famous students, including Judah ha-Nasi, the man who compiled many of Simeon's aphorisms. Simeon was sent as an emissary to Rome, where he pleaded for the Jewish cause and succeeded in lifting the Catholic Church's sanctions on many Jewish observances.

There is an interesting story about the events in Rome during Rabbi Simeon's visit. The Roman emperor's daughter had become mentally ill, and the emperor was frantically looking for a cure. Rabbi Simeon offered to help. Within a few days, the daughter became well, and the emperor was so happy that he promised to give Rabbi Simeon anything he asked for. That is when the Rabbi asked for the decrees against the Jews to be abolished.

Simeon believed and preached total devotion to studying and understanding the Torah. He emphasized the importance of focusing on the spirit in which any civil law or rituals were performed and not following the given the word blindly. He believed that when laws and rituals are performed and followed based on the spirit in which they were written, then their application can be modified suitably depending on the situation.

Rabbi Simeon is revered as one of the greatest scholars and teachers of Kabbalah law and ethics, with his love and attachment to the Torah and Talmud mirrored in many of his sayings and proverbs. Once, he was believed to have said, "*If I was the one receiving these holy words from God Himself at Mount Sinai, then I would have prayed for two months. One for the continuous study of the sacred texts and another one for eating.*" But then again, he admitted it would have been a mistake if he had asked for such a thing. He said that with one mouth, we humans say so many wrong things. Imagine how many more incorrect ways of speech we would use if we had two mouths instead of one.

Simeon is believed to have performed multiple miracles. He lived the life of an ascetic and dedicated his entire life to the growth and development of Kabbalah. Rabbi Simeon is believed to have died in Meron, a village near Safed. Even today, pilgrims visit and pray at his tomb every year on the anniversary of his death.

These aspects of Simeon's personality are perhaps why the authorship of the Zohar is attributed to him. However, most modern scholars ascribe the Zohar authorship to Moses de Leon, a Jewish mystic of the 13th century.

Moses de Leon - Moses de Leon's original name was Moses Ben Shem. He was born in Spain. He was a Jewish Kabbalist, and most scholars believe he was the author of the Zohar. The details of Moses de Leon's life history are obscure. He lived in Guadalajara, which was the Spanish center of Kabbalists until 1290. After that, he traveled widely until he settled in Avila.

He met Isaac ben Samuel of Acre, a Palestinian Kabbalist in Valladolid in northwestern Spain. Moses is believed to have told him he held the original, centuries-old manuscript of the Zohar. This was recorded in Isaac's diary. The copies of the original were in circulation since the 1280s. Considering the antiquity of the manuscript and that it was authored by Simeon ben Yohai, its value and interest to Isaac of Acre was incomparable.

Sadly, Moses passed away before he could show the original manuscript to Isaac. Further, Isaac heard that Moses' wife denied the original manuscript's existence and said that her husband wrote the Zohar. Another reason scholars believe that Moses wrote the Zohar is there is evidence of the influence of Joseph Gikatilla, another Spanish Kabbalist and a contemporary and friend of Moses de Leon. Gikatilla authored a book titled Ginnat Egoz (or Nut Orchard), which appears to be the source of vital terminology used in the Zohar.

These influences were recognized by Gershom Scholem, a highly influential 20th-century scholar of Jewish mysticism. He was convinced that the Zohar was a work of the Medieval Era and was not of 2nd-century antiquity. Scholem also compared the Zohar with Moses' other work and identified that Moses was indeed the author of the Zohar.

Scholem said that Moses wrote the Zohar to counter the rise of rationalism among the Spanish Jewish community during that time and re-establish the supremacy of traditional religion. The Zohar attempted to give Kabbalah rituals and doctrines a new and refreshing reinterpretation.

And yet, many scholars still believe that the Zohar was authored by the 2nd-century Kabbalist, Simeon ben Yohai. The ones in favor of the Zohar being written by Simeon ben Yohai use the following arguments:

Great Kabbalists such as Shlomo Alkabetz, Moses Cordovero, Isaac Luria, Joseph Caro, Moses Luzzato, and many more agree that the Zohar was written by Rabbi Simeon ben Yohai. And for these Kabbalists, the Zohar was more than merely a field of study. It was a way of life for such people. And they argue that the person who wrote the Zohar should have had the same level of spirituality as the contents of the book. Only Simeon ben Yohai fits the bill.

After Rabbi Moses, many other Kabbalists influenced Kabbalah. Some important ones include:

Isaac, the Blind - Believed to have lived in the 13th century, Isaac the Blind was a well-known Kabbalist from Provence, Southern France. He is believed to have been one of the earliest scholars who dedicated his entire life to the study of Kabbalah and its teachings.

His most significant contribution was the introduction of a particular type of meditation focusing on the ten sefirot. According to Isaac, anyone who tried to meditate on the sefirot could ascend to heaven and become one with Ein Sof. Even today, his techniques are practiced in sefirot meditation.

Moses Cordovero - Rabbi Moses Cordovero lived in the 16th century and was an influential Kabbalist in Safed. He is most famous for his work, "Pardes Rimonim," which translates to "The Pomegranate Orchard." In this work, Rabbi Moses Cordovero brought together the most extant Kabbalistic teachings and sacred texts. He refined and explained the ten sefirot. Rabbi Moses' work was later incorporated by his student Isaac Luria, who revolutionized Kabbalah teachings.

Isaac Luria - The most critical contribution of Rabbi Isaac Luria to Kabbalah was introducing the "tsimtsum" concept. This idea is about "God's withdrawal" to allow the creation or emergence of another manifestation. His "withdrawal" was a crucial element in the creation process. His vastness consumed everything, and he "withdrew" or "stepped back" to make room for the creation of the world.

Rabbi Isaac Luria's influence on Kabbalistic teaching was so profound and strong that modern Kabbalists refer to his ideas as "Lurianic Kabbalah," giving him a special place in the realm of Kabbalah.

The Language and Structure of the Zohar

Much of the Zohar was written in an unfamiliar form of literary Aramaic, the vernacular spoken in the region where Rabbi Simeon came from. The Zohar consists of mystical commentaries on the Five Books of Moses, collectively called the Pentateuch. Simeon ben Yohai and his disciples (or companions) had a series of discussions and dialogues against the background of an imaginary Palestine. The dialogues are centered on the ten sefirot or the idea that God manifested Himself in 10 ascending emanations.

When Simeon and his son, Elazar, were taking refuge from Roman persecution in a secluded cave for 13 years, they were visited by the Prophet Elijah twice a day. It was Prophet Elijah who revealed the contents of the Zohar to Rabbi Simeon. The Zohar contains a commentary on the Bible and has multiple sections, of which the primary section is the Sefer ha Zohar. The Sefer ha Zohar deals with the weekly portion of the Torah and has these attachments:

- **Idra Rabbah or the Great Assembly** - This was written after Rabbi Simeon and his son came out of seclusion. They selected eight disciples who, along with Simeon and Elazar, formed the Great Assembly. In this section, the hidden, esoteric teachings of the Torah were explained.

- **Sifra diTzenuta or the Book of the Veiled Mystery** - This section deals with the creative process structure.

- **Sitrei Torah or the Secrets of the Torah** - This section deals with the power of the divine names and examines how this power can be harnessed to access the infinite cosmic power.

- **Idra Zuta or the Lesser Assembly** - This deals with Rabbi Simeon's teachings not dealt with in the Idra Rabbah. It was revealed on the day of Rabbi Simeon's death.

- **Ra'aya Mehemna or The Faithful Shepherd** - This section deals with those teachings and precepts not part of the daily discussions between prophet Elijah and Rabbi Simeon.

- **Midrash haNe'elam or The Recondite Exposition** - This section deals with Jewish numerology. It contains a vast collection of permutations and combinations of the Hebrew numerals and the Aleph Beth, the Hebrew letters.

- **Zohar Hadash or The New Zohar** - This is an independent commentary that includes the Torah and The Song of Songs, the Five Scrolls (Megillot), Lamentations, Ruth, Esther, and Ecclesiastes.

- **Tikunei Zohar or Emendations of the Zohar** - This section deals with teachings related to the Age of Aquarius and the general teachings in the Zohar.

- **Tosefta or Additions** - This section has a few supplements to the Zohar referring to the ten sefirot.

The Hebrew Language

Kabbalists believe that the Hebrew language was given to humankind by God. In Genesis, it is written that God created the cosmos by pronouncing His Divine Will. In Kabbalah, this is interpreted as the language being the ultimate source of creative power. In "Sefer Yetzirah," the creation process is described as having taken place with 22 Hebrew alphabets and ten cardinal numbers.

In the early days, "Sefer Yetzirah" was interpreted with magical orientations. The ancient Kabbalists who read this text were able to perceive explanations that showed how they could imagine and perhaps even repeat the creation process by manipulating the 22 Hebrew alphabets. The text explained how to create a "golem," an animated being created from an inanimate object (an ancient Jewish folklore idea) using the 22 Hebrew alphabets. In the same way, it would be possible to destroy the "golem" by manipulating the Hebrew alphabet. The power of the Hebrew language is an essential aspect of Kabbalah.

Even today, many interesting aspects of the Hebrew language are not common knowledge. Let us look at a few of these:

• Hebrew is considered a sacred language ("lashon hakodesh"), and many people use it only for prayer.

• Although originally it was a biblical language, today it has been revived and spoken as a contemporary language in the modern world. Interestingly, although it was not spoken commonly, the written form continued to be used for centuries without a break.

• Hebrew alphabets are written right to left. Hebrew numbers are written left to right.

• The Hebrew alphabet is an "abjad," a writing system that allows the reader to choose the correct vowel. Although Hebrew has vowels, they are not marked, and you have to know how each word is pronounced before you can read.

Other Important Texts of Kabbalah

According to Kabbalists, besides the Zohar, a few other texts shaped the Kabbalah, including:

Sefer Yetzirah or the Book of Formation - This is the earliest extant work on Jewish mysticism. It is also the only work that finds a mention in the Talmud. Traditionalists believe that Sefer Yetzirah was written by Abraham himself, although others believe that it was passed down orally from Abraham and was recorded by Rabbi Akiva. The Kabbalists see Sefer Yetzirah as being shrouded in mystery, even though its importance is not diminished by its mysterious, and often undecipherable, nature.

Sefer Habahir or the Book of Brightness - Kabbalists attribute this book's authorship to Rabbi Nechunya ben Hakannah, a Kabbalah and Talmudic mystic who lived in the first century. It was the first book to discuss the ten sefirot as ten divine emanations of God, which was expanded in the Zohar by Rabbi Simeon in the 2nd century. Sefer Habahir also discusses soul incarnation (or gilgulim), interpretation of the Hebrew alphabets, the various divine names of God, and explains numerous mitzvahs (divine commandments that have to be performed as duties).

The Growth and Development of Kabbalah

The wisdom of the Zohar was not aligned with the consciousness of the times it was written in. Its contents were disharmonious with the intellect and physical condition of those times because the Zohar's was a powerful physical energy source. Many modern scholars believe that the Zohar can be compared to a powerful source of electrical energy.

And therefore, until the human world was ready to embrace this powerful source of physical and intellectual energy, it had to be kept safely hidden. If it were unleashed when the human world was not ready for it, then not only would the knowledge in it be useless, but it could also be dangerous. The Zohar was kept hidden for more than a thousand years, which Rabbi Simeon predicted.

In the 13th century, the Zohar came into the possession of Moses de Leon, the famous Spanish Kabbalist, even though how he got the possession remains a mystery. According to legends, Rabbi Simeon found the Zohar in the cave where Rabbi Simeon had hidden it, believed to be the same one in which he and his son lived for 13 years to escape Roman persecution.

Regardless of this mysterious and unknown aspect, one thing is certain. When Rabbi Moses transcribed the Zohar, Spain became the hub of the study and practice of Kabbalah. Multiple abridged and incomplete copies appeared over the next two centuries after its discovery by Moses.

The Zohar and its teachings quickly spread to Italy and other parts of Western Europe, but it took longer to move to Eastern Europe. After the Jews were expelled from Spain in 1492, they leaned on the Zohar to understand and interpret mystical speculations. The influence of the Zohar was felt by the Jewish community many centuries after it was composed. Rabbi Isaac Luria, who lived between 1534 and 1572, is credited with starting the Golden Age of Kabbalistic Study, which peaked in the 16th and 17th centuries. Rabbi Luria was introduced to Zohar when he was a teenager living in Cairo, Egypt, with his family.

Rabbi Luria was so moved by what he read he spent many years in deep contemplation and meditation on the text in which he had multiple revelations from Simeon, Elazar, and Akiva. Rabbi Luria then moved to Safed, a Galilean village where a large Kabbalistic community flourished under the able leadership of Rabbi Moses Cordovero.

He lived in Safed for the remainder of his life as a highly influential and visionary scholar whose insights helped explain and systemize Zohar's basic concepts. All of Luria's teachings were transcribed by his disciple, Rabbi Chaim Vital. In the 16th century, Rabbi Abraham Azulai proclaimed that the basic concepts of Kabbalah must be disseminated to everyone, young and old, because he said that eliminating war, hatred, and enmity among humans would end when the world read and understood the Zohar. Moreover, the Zohar itself mentions that even young children can grasp the inner meaning and truths of Kabbalah.

Slowly again, with the advent of the Scientific Revolution, faith in esoteric and spiritual knowledge began to fade, and the decreasing belief in Kabbalah reached new depths by the end of the 19th century. Right through the 20th century, the Jews in America had a highly secular outlook on life, believing that the advancements made in science and technology were eliminating the "darkness of religion." They believed that improved self-understanding among humans and increased objective and scientific perspectives would make us increasingly humane and that religion created unnecessary divides.

Then, World War II happened, which resulted in an unprecedented loss of human life and unbelievable levels of demonic behavior by humans. For example, the horrors of Auschwitz originated in Germany, a country that produced many Nobel Prize winners in different scientific fields. The horrors of Hiroshima and Nagasaki were the terrible outcome of scientific advancement. And as a final straw on the camel's back, the discovery and spread of nuclear power that many nations had access to resulted in a constant global conflict which, if not controlled, could have resulted in hitherto unimagined disasters for the entire human race.

Such challenges in the field of science drove thinkers to ancient wisdom and teachings once considered esoteric and difficult to understand. And along with Indian mysticism, Buddhism, Sufism, and other oriental belief systems, Kabbalah was also revived through the revival of the Zohar.

The Zohar is not just any book. It is "the holy book," and every letter and word in it is sacred and is related to the divine. The Zohar contains and expresses all aspects of life in the cosmos. When we study the Zohar, we pay homage to the Creator and His entire Creation.

As you read and delve deep into the spirituality of the Zohar, you will notice three yet interwoven elements, and these three include:

- One element of the Zohar is that it is a commentary on the Bible. It discusses the characters, narratives, laws, genealogies, and descriptive passages from the Bible.

- The second element discussed in the Zohar is the spiritual landscape that has developed not only from the time of creation but even before that right until this present moment.

- And the last element of the Zohar is that it is a vast collection of useful, practical tools and instruction manuals to help humans with the journey through the spiritual landscape to transform in such a way as to achieve the true purpose of our lives.

Discovering the tools and instructions requires a detailed reading and understanding of the obscure messages hidden between the lines. It is vital that you should not restrict the learning of Kabbalah to mere theory. You should incorporate what you have learned into your life and put these lessons into action. Ultimately, the Zohar is not about learning lessons but a directed and clear call to action.

Learning and imbibing the power of the Zohar can be compared to building a strong, deep bond of friendship. For example, recall how your relationship with your best friend started and developed. When you first met him, you only recognized him through his physical appearance. As you didn't know his deeper feelings and thoughts, your expectations of him were limited too. It is likely that your uncertainty about your new friend made you wary about him at the beginning of the relationship.

As your relationship with your friend deepened, you slowly learned about his feelings, thoughts, and deep intentions too. This change could take years to happen, or sometimes, if you met him every day, it could happen sooner. The ultimate thing is to be able to see your friend's spiritual and inner aspects besides his physical appearance.

Interestingly, once you have connected with your friend at a deeper level, then his physical appearance becomes irrelevant. You may not see or interact with him for days, and yet, the connection remains strong. Even absent his physical form, your emotional and spiritual bonds are more than sufficient to keep the relationship strong.

The same thing can be said about the Zohar too. You first connect with the physical text, the commentaries, and the descriptions. Your initial connection with the holy book will not relate to the stories and parables from the Torah. Then, you move toward finding the deeper meaning that the sacred book is trying to reveal to you. With each movement forward in your understanding of the Zohar, you get closer to God until finally, you feel at one with Him.

Chapter Two: Other Books of Zohar

This chapter is dedicated to the other books of the Zohar after the commentaries on the Torah.

The Book of the Hidden or Sifra diTzni'utal

The Book of the Hidden, also called the Book of Concealment, is a small book, just three pages long. As the name suggests, its meaning is cryptic and veiled. Kabbalists believe this book represents the most distilled part of the Zohar. Similar to Sefer Yetzirah, especially in its anatomy and enumerations, the Book of the Hidden is written with hints (called *remazim* in Hebrew) and suggestions of divine characteristics.

Although on the face of it, this 5-chapter book explains the seminal verses in Genesis through enigmatic poetry, at a deeper level, the knowledge and wisdom in it form the foundation of Kabbalah. Each of the five chapters is contained in one brief paragraph and represents all the wisdom of Kabbalah. It is described as the "little book that holds much."

The Book of the Hidden has a veiled description of God's body. Interestingly, it focuses on God's beard. Within the few pages, this book holds the crux of Kabbalah. It explains how the divine breath gives life to everything in the cosmos. It also talks about another important element of Kabbalah, namely the synergy between male and female energies needed to maintain balance in the universe.

The Great Assembly or the Idra Rabba

The word "Idra" translates to the sitting positions of wise sages, which are usually circular. The word "Rabba" means "Great." Meaning the Idra Rabba or the Great Assembly. In this section of the Zohar, discussions take place between nine disciples (students) under the leadership of Rashbi or Rabbi Simeon ben Yohai. These nine are:

- Rabbi Eleazar, son of Rashbi
- Rabbi Abba
- Rabbi Yehuda
- Rabbi Yossi bar Yaakov
- Rabbi Yitzchak
- Rabbi Chezkiyah bar Rav
- Rabbi Chiyya
- Rabbi Yossi
- Rabbi Yisa

In the Idra Rabba, the discussions start with Rabbi Simeon's opening words. After this, each of the nine sages rises and talks about the secret of the Divinity. Rabbi Simeon either responds or adds to the words spoken by each of the nine sages. An unexpected episode occurs before the assembly is broken up.

Three , including Rabbi Yossi bar Yaakov, Rabbi Chezkiyah bar Rav, and Rabbi Yisa, die. As described in the Idra Rabba, after they breathed their last breath, these students traveled to the eternal world swathed in a divine light. The remaining students and Rabbi Simeon watched their three companions taken to their heavenly abode by angels.

This sight filled their hearts with fear and uncertainty. Rabbi Simeon spoke a few words and calmed their minds. Rabbi Simeon said, "Perhaps their death is a warning to us and a divine punishment for revealing and talking about something that was kept hidden since the time it was heard for the first time by Moses on Mount Sinai."

A heavenly voice spoke in response to Rabbi Simeon's words, "You and your companions are fortunate, Rabbi Simeon, because what has been revealed to you has not been revealed to all."

The Smaller Assembly or the Idra Zuta

The word "Zuta" means "smaller or fewer," which differentiates this section of the Zohar from the Idra Rabba, considering the assembly had three members less. In this part of the Zohar, Rabbi Simeon and his remaining companions meet again and continue their discussions.

Ra'aya Meheimna or The Faithful Shepherd

The Faithful Shepherd is the largest book of the Zohar. It is a collection of the teachings of Moses, the Faithful Shepherd, which he taught and revealed to Rabbi Simeon, his companions, and to Tannaim and Amoraim, the great sages whose teachings are recorded in Talmudic literature.

This assembly of Holy Friends took place in Beit Midrash, the Jewish school of Rabbi Simeon ben Yohai. It contains the secrets and teachings about the mitzvot (laws and commandments) of the Torah. The Torah mitzvot are described, explained, and clarified. The roots and the deep meanings of the mitzvot are explained in the Ra'aya Meheimna.

The Ra'aya Meheimna was originally a vast book with commentaries and explanations of all the 613 mitzvot. Some eminent rabbis have tried to collect the Faithful Shepherd's entire texts and organize its contents under two categories - negative and positive commandments.

In the Zohar, the text of the Ra'aya Meheimna is spread across several parts. Some of this section can be found on separate pages, while others are woven into other sections of the book. The texts of this section are found in volumes 2 and 3. It is not found explicitly in volume 1.

The Hidden Midrash or Midrash haNe'elam

The sections related to the Hidden Midrash is so-called because it deals with matters about the higher levels of the soul. The language used in this text is a mixture of Hebrew and Aramaic, sometimes separately, and sometimes both languages together. It discusses the nature of the soul, the work of creation, etc.

Besides the above primary sections and texts, the Zohar has sections of a different nature and importance. For example, there are texts collectively called "Assembly of the House of the Tabernacle" or Idra deVei Mashkana dealing with the meanings and secrets of prayers.

The Heikhalot or "Palaces" describes the palaces of the Garden of Eden and those in Gehinnom. In Raza de Razin, or "Secret of Secrets, the essence of man is described using the features of his hands and face. The section of "The Elder on Statutes" or Saba deMishpatim deals with punishments of the body when it is in the grave and talks about the transmigration of the soul.

The Zohar contains all knowledge and wisdom needed to lead not only a meaningful and fulfilling life of compassion and kindness but also that which can help you transcend the materialistic world to unite with God.

Chapter Three: Zohar - The Book of Radiance

Now that you have a good idea about Zohar and its place in Kabbalah specifically and the world of spirituality, it is time to move into the contents of this sacred text. If you read the original text, then you will find what is discussed in this chapter.

Zohar is called the Book of Radiance. One of the most interesting aspects of this book is that it is written using a technique called "automatic writing." In this seemingly bizarre technique, the author does not stop to think. Instead, he or she writes as if in a trance and transcribes whatever comes to the mind. This technique helps to retrieve those ideas deeply buried in the subconscious mind (believed to be put there by God Himself) and is considered to be a format that helps the writer to be closest to his or her divinity.

Incidentally, the word Ein Sof is used for God throughout the text of the Zohar. Ein Sof translates to "Infinite," and this phrase is more aligned with the Kabbalistic viewpoint of the divine being unknowable and beyond the limits of human understanding. Against the conventional terminology of God, which reflects a knowable and tangible being who resides in heaven, Ein Sof reflects such a powerful and deep entity that humans can only grasp fragments of, and that too, only through profound, beyond-human mystical experiences.

The word "Zohar" translates to "shining" or radiance." The name is quite paradoxical considering that the contents are shrouded in mystic obscurity. The obscurity is not only because of the "partially invented" Aramaic dialect in which it is written but also because of the depth of esotericism it contains.

Moreover, each of the Aramaic letters, numbers, and words in the Zohar is believed to have so much power they are considered the very building blocks of Creation. The power of the language is believed to include human speech, which influences our physical and spiritual worlds, and divine speech, which continues to create and will continue to create a new world each new day. Therefore, neither the language nor the contents are easy to unravel and understand.

And translating it into English and other languages was an even more arduous task. In 2017, Stanford University Press came out with an English translation of the Zohar and commentaries by highly eminent Kabbalistic scholars and researchers such as Daniel Matt from Berkeley. Daniel Matt spent over 18 years researching for this project and combed through early manuscripts and rare, printed works using what he was able to first create an Aramaic text. He then used this Aramaic text to translate the book into English that was both readable and easy to understand.

Daniel Matt's work consists of 12 volumes, and each is hundreds of pages in length. The Zohar is a massive book. The contents of the Zohar can help people connect with the divine. It can help a dedicated student connect with something beyond human limitations. Its teachings are not just powerful but also dangerous. This is why Kabbalists, at one point in history, laid a rule that only married men above the age of 40 should be allowed to read and learn it.

Another reason the Zohar remained lost in history was there were no good translations available. The only way you could read the Zohar would be if you knew Aramaic, and in addition, you were familiar with the old, partially invented one. Thanks to Daniel Matt, the mysteries of the Zohar can be accessed by any interested student across the globe.

The Zohar tries to answer existential questions provocatively and enigmatically. The Zohar, in its own unique way, tries to capture the imagination of readers. By keeping us hooked onto its more visceral rather than literal expositions, the Zohar helps us get lost in the ethereal world of our imagination, leaving us more room to connect with our subconscious mind, a place closer to divinity than the physical world.

For example, God's description in the Zohar is radical and nothing like the God who sits on a golden throne in heaven. Called Ein Sof, God in the Zohar is described with both male and female traits. This divine being is beyond gender and is infinite and boundless.

Translating the Zohar was challenging for multiple reasons, according to Daniel Matt. Besides having tools to break down the intellectual and language-based enigma in it, he had to explore and unravel his own spiritual and the mental world to connect with the Zohar and make sense of what was being said in it.

Before Daniel Matt did the complete translation, bits and pieces of the book were translated into English. For example, Margo Pritzker, the lady who funded Daniel Matt's humongous work, was trying to learn the Zohar from an incomplete translated version. Both were unhappy this work skipped difficult, complex, and erotic passages, and they agreed that the Zohar requires a full and unabridged English translation. Daniel Matt then started his work under the patronage of the Pritzker family.

The Zohar weaves tales of rabbis traveling together, unraveling the mysteries of the Torah and other ancient texts. Through these intricately woven tales, ancient scriptures are interpreted and discussed with such remarkable depth that every Jewish ritual takes on a new spiritual resonance that goes beyond blind ritualism. The Zohar creates a new and fulfilling version of the Torah and the biblical stories, events, and characters.

Let us take the example of the Sabbath. The average Jew thinks of the Sabbath as a rest day. However, in the Zohar, the Sabbath becomes God's bride, and the Jews host the angels who have come along with the bride at their dinner table, which becomes a wedding feast. In the Zohar, Abraham is not just a patriarch but a representative of divine love. His compassion flows seamlessly into the world and springs forth new life. Similarly, according to the Zohar, the Torah is not merely God's commanded word. It is an oral incarnation of Him which has the power to bring to life the divinity in those with the heart and mind to engage with it.

Another interesting story in the Zohar is the story of the Garden of Eden. In the biblical story, God expels Adam for being disobedient. In the Zohar, the question "Who expelled who?" is prompted. So, this startling question makes the readers think. So, if God didn't expel Adam, then did Adam expel God? For the uninitiated, this might look like a sacrilegious statement. When you put your mind to it, it holds a profound lesson for all of us.

By "expelling" God from the Garden of Eden, Adam (representing humans) pushed God out of his life. Through this question, we realize that we have disconnected ourselves from our divinity. And the best of the Zohar is that it teaches you how to recover that divinity and the lost knowledge.

Also, the language of the Zohar is love and eros. Here is an example of how the Zohar explains the relationship between the Torah and its students in terms of being a romantic relationship. "*The Torah is a beautiful woman who has a secret lover. The lover keeps circling around her gates out of his love for her. And she, knowing that her lover is trying to seek her out, opens a window, shows her face for an instant, and quickly shuts it again. No one else but the lover sees her, and the love flows between them. Torah reveals herself only to her true lover, the one whose heart yearns to know more about her love and get lost in it. She beckons the lover with a slight hint which only he can decipher and open the floodgates of love."*

According to the Zohar, love is the eternal element that binds the cosmos. Love brings together all the dualities in the universe, including light and dark, heaven and earth, male and female, etc. The Song of Solomon is discussed in the Zohar. The lush, rich gardens described in the Song of Solomon are conceptualized as a place of sacred love. It includes the erotic aspects of love too.

The Jews worshipped the female aspect of divinity and yet did not venerate celibacy or virginity. Torah was the bride of God and of Israel in a spiritually consummated sense. The esotericism in the Zohar was a deliberate design to enhance its mystery. The depths of imagery enhanced the imagination of the Kabbalists, and they often chanted the mantra-like Zohar verses to be inspired by the beauty of sound that resonated with the frequency of the person who chants.

Simeon ben Yohai and Disciples

Rabbi Simeon ben Yohai is also called Rashbi. His name is also spelled as Rabbi Shimon bar Yohai. The sacred Zohar describes the journey of Rabbi Simeon ben Yohai and his companions or disciples as they traveled through Galilee, the former kingdom of Israel, and currently in the northern parts of Palestine. Right through their journey, the rabbi and his companions discussed their interpretations of the Torah, focusing on the main characters. These characters from the Torah become a part of the Zohar's narrative, and they kept coming in and leaving the group headed by Rabbi Simeon. The disciples also entered and exited the group seamlessly, even while moving from one character to another.

Why was Rabbi Simeon chosen? This aspect is discussed through many parables and stories in the Zohar. Rabbi Simeon lived a fugitive and solitary life for many years. The physical limitation and constraints that are part of such a life usually impede spiritual progress, and attaining higher levels of spiritual consciousness in such situations is difficult. Rabbi Simeon overcame these impediments and transcended the laws of space and time, and knew and experienced the root cause of all existence even in the most trying of circumstances.

It is vital to point out here that the contents of the Zohar were not revealed exclusively to Rabbi Simeon and that no one before him knew about it. His revered teacher, Rabbi Akiva, and many before him were well-versed and highly knowledgeable in the wisdom of Kabbalah.

The teachings of Kabbalah were revealed on Mount Sinai in Israel in oral form. The ones who understood the dazzling truth and the power of these teachings could not teach it or make others understand, considering that they were esoteric and clothed in rich, sometimes confusing language. The average man had to wait for Rabbi Simeon's arrival to write the Zohar down to understand the powerful teachings of the Kabbalah.

Many themes have an important place in Zohar. The sacred book discusses:

- The cosmos, its creation
- The nature of evil and sin
- The nature of God
- God's relationship with the human world
- God's attributes (or the ten sefirot)
- Commentaries on the Torah
- Kabbalah holidays
- The commandments,

- Prayer and rituals
- The role of priests
- The experience of exile

These themes are handled in the next section of this book. Let us look at a few of these themes briefly here.

Commentaries on the Torah - The Zohar can be considered a narrative of wandering mystics led by a master. These wandering mystics discussed and interpreted the Torah in various ways as they traveled from place to place in the Holy Land. The concept of traveling is seen as a way of freeing their imaginations, thereby empowering the travelers to delve deep into their minds and discuss the deepest and most mysterious aspects of the Torah.

The Zohar's purpose is deeper than that of the other Kabbalah works. The Zohar's primary intention is to reveal the true, hidden meaning of the Torah. Each of the biblical characters and parables is symbolized as souls or parts of the divine.

The Ten Sefirot - The nature of God, who is called Ein Sof (or the Limitless One), is one of the major themes in the Zohar. These elements appear in other earlier Kabbalah mystical texts. The sefirot are believed to be emanations or expressions of the divine. They are part of the divine and the elements which Ein Sof used to relate and connect with the human world. The ten sefirot (listed below) form a framework in which humans can have a spiritual experience.

- Keter - Crown
- Hokhmah - Wisdom
- Binah - Understanding
- Hesed - Mercy
- Din - Justice
- Tiferet - Beauty
- Nezah - Eternity

- Hod - Glory

- Yesod - Foundation

- Shekhinah - the female aspect of the divine. Shekinah is also called Malchut or Royalty

The purpose of the Zohar is to help us achieve spiritual unity with the divine through contemplation. The spiritual contemplation practices explained in the Zohar appear to take on an erotic character as the relationship between God, and the mystic is described as a lover's relationship. God is the bride, and the mystic or seeker is the man who seeks union with his lover through study, meditation, and prayer. These practices help the seeker to lose himself in the divine, a state called devekut (or attachment to God). Also, the metaphor of sexual union and birth is used in the Zohar to symbolize the union of the seeker with God, his bride, and his birth as a new person.

Chapter Four: From Genesis to Deuteronomy

The Zohar is a collection of volumes that deals with multiple Kabbalah concepts (already discussed briefly in the previous chapters). Here, we will look at each "book" of the Zohar in a little more detail.

Zohar and the Torah

The first part of Zohar is called Zohar al' ha Torah or Zohar on the Torah (the First Five Books of Moses). This earlier part of the Zohar comprises several small books published in three volumes:

- The first volume is on the Genesis

- The second volume is on Exodus

- The third volume is on Leviticus, Numbers, and Deuteronomy

Genesis, Exodus, Leviticus, Numbers, and Deuteronomy make up the Five Books of Moses or the Torah. The Zohar discusses four types of interpretations of biblical verses in the Torah, namely:

- Peshat or the literal meaning

- Remez or the illusionary interpretation

- Derash or the anagogical interpretation

- Sod or the mystical meaning

The initial letters of the four words "Peshat," Remez," "Derash," and "Sod" combine to form PARDES or Paradise. Achieving paradise or union with the divine is the ultimate aim of any Kabbalist. As is obvious, the mystical interpretation is the highest form of interpretation and is the most difficult to understand.

These four interpretations are formed based on Zohar's premise that all the visible things that humans can see, sense, and experience are part of the exoteric reality. Over and above this visible phenomenon, there exists an esoteric reality which aims to teach and show humans those things which are not visible to us.

This principle is the basis of the Zohar because it says that the divine being is shown to us through a gradation of emanations, and we can see the mark of divinity in each emanation. We ascend through the gradations until we recognize, identify, and reach the cause of all causes.

Climbing up through the gradations takes time and persistence and will happen only after the mind has gone through and grasped the four stages of knowledge and intelligence, including:

- The knowledge of the exoteric or the external world as we see, sense, and experience it. The Zohar explains this vision as seeing things through a mirror that uses indirect lighting.

- The knowledge of the essence of all things in the external world. The Zohar describes this vision as that which is seen through a mirror that uses direct lighting.

- The intuitive knowledge

- The knowledge of love - The true meaning of the Zohar cannot be seen or experienced by those who don't love it.

When one gains knowledge through love, then this individual can achieve ecstatic states, which are possible only with holy visions. The Zohar describes a contemplative posture to achieve this ecstatic state as follows, "*The practitioner has to remain completely still with his hands between his knees. In this position, he should be absorbed in murmuring prayers, hymns, and in deep contemplation.*"

The Zohar describes seven ecstatic states, each of which is seen in a different color. At each of the seven stages, the practitioner reaches a different-colored heavenly hall (or hekal). The hekal of the final and seventh stage is colorless, and this stage marks the end of his contemplation and the beginning of his subconscious state.

Bereishit - Genesis

The first book of the Torah, Genesis, is called Bereishit in Hebrew, which translates to "In the beginning." It begins with the description of creation by God in six days. He created Adam and Eve on the sixth day and gave them the beautiful Garden of Eden to live in. However, they sinned by eating the forbidden fruit and were expelled from there. Next, Cain, son of Adam and Eve, kills his brother, Abel, and the world is thrown into chaos.

After ten generations, God restarts the world by flooding it. But before that, He orders Noah, the only good man during that time, to build an Ark to save himself and one pair of each of the living species. When the flood ends, Noah's descendants, in their arrogance, build the Tower of Babel to reach the sky. God destroys this tower and creates confusion by making everyone gathered to speak in different languages so that no one could understand the other.

Ten generations after Noah, Abraham is introduced in the Bible, and he is commanded to follow God to the promised land of Israel. He proves his faith in God by overcoming many obstacles and tests that God put before him. Sadly, Abraham's wife, Sarah, could not give him a child because she was barren.

She tells Abraham to marry Hagar, her maid who has a son named Ishmael. Then, God advises Abraham to circumcise himself, after which Sarah gives birth to a boy named Isaac. When Isaac was born, Abraham was 100 years, and Sarah was 90 years. As a final proof of his faith, God asked Abraham to sacrifice Isaac. Abraham gets ready for the sacrifice, but God stops him at the last minute.

Isaac marries Rebecca, and they have twin sons named Esau (the elder) and Jacob. Jacob is studious, whereas Esau is a hunter. Isaac wants to bless his elder son, Esau, but Rebecca thinks Jacob deserves the blessings. So, she makes him take his elder brother's place and receive the blessings from Isaac, after which he runs away to his uncle's house to escape Esau's anger.

His uncle Laban gave Jacob in marriage to his two daughters, Rachel and Leah. Jacob becomes prosperous, and on God's commands, returned to the Holy Land, and even makes up with his brother, Esau.

Jacob had 12 sons, his favorite being Joseph. The other 11 got jealous and sold Joseph to slave traders. As a slave, Joseph landed in Egypt, and there he became rich and prosperous. But again, misfortune visited him because he was thrown in jail for unfair reasons because he refused the overtures of his master's wife.

Joseph was freed from jail to interpret the Pharaoh's dreams. Joseph predicted a long period of plenty to be followed by a famine. Joseph was appointed as the viceroy and was given the responsibility of preparing for the famine. People from far and near approached Joseph for food when the famine finally arrived.

His brothers were among the supplicants, although they couldn't recognize him. Joseph was angry at them for their earlier behavior. So, he tortured them for a while before revealing his identity to them, and there was a happy family reunion. The entire family settled in Egypt at Joseph's behest. He lived happily for 17 years with his big family. He blessed his children before his death and asked that he be buried in Canaan next to his parents.

Genesis begins with the creation of the cosmos and slowly narrows its focus onto a small group of people, with Abraham leading the pack. Abraham's legacy shaped the future of humankind.

Shemot - Exodus

The events described in the Book of the Exodus took place 400 years after the death of Joseph, his brothers, and the Pharaoh, who patronized them. It describes the journey of the Israelites from Egypt to Canaan, as commanded by God under Moses' leadership.

Joseph's descendants had grown in large numbers, and the new Egyptian leaders felt threatened by their growing numbers and popularity. So, they subdued the Israelites through cruel laws. All Israelites were forced into slavery, and Hebrew baby boys were to be drowned in the Nile River.

Israeli women resisted these cruel laws, and one of them found the courage to set her newborn son afloat in a basket so he could be saved from death. This baby was found by the Pharaoh's daughter, who raised him. This child was Moses.

He was forced to flee from Egypt after killing an Egyptian soldier mercilessly whipping an Israeli worker. Moses ran away to Midian, a small town near the foothills of Mount Sinai. Here, he married the daughter of Jethro, a priest, and lived the life of a shepherd.

God wanted Moses to release the suffering of the Israelites in Egypt. He appeared before Moses in the form of a burning bush and commanded him to return to Egypt so he could lead the Israelites back to Canaan, the land with flowing milk and honey. God presented a magical staff to Moses. Moses and Aaron, his brother, left for Egypt, where he organized the Israelis together and confronted the Pharaoh. But the Pharaoh did not heed Moses' warning, despite his many miracles.

Moses led the Israelites out of Egypt after many years in which God sent plagues and famines to Egypt to show his support for those who believed in Him. After many struggles, which included dealing with believers and non-believers, all helped by God, Moses led them to Mount Sinai, where God sent His messages (including the ten commandments) to the people through Moses.

Not all Israelites believed in Him. Many disregarded God's commandments and rules. God punished them so they would understand His power, and they lived a morally uplifting life so that ultimately the people He loved could rejoin the divine.

The Exodus also includes multiple laws and commandments that God sent to His people through Moses. The Exodus explains the origin of the Torah and its laws and commandments. Yet, Exodus is more than a compilation of laws. It described a way of life that takes us closer to God.

The tradition of the Exodus is replete with symbols that present God's promise to the Israelites. Social laws and festivals like the humane treatment of slaves and rituals like the Passover were passed on to the people through the word of God.

The Zohar's interpretation of the Exodus and how the exiled but freed Israelites went with Moses to Canaan filled, with milk and honey, go deeper than merely as a story of God helping believers. The Zohar explains that the worst exile for humans is not knowing and acknowledging God's presence.

Egypt was the ultimate symbol of this exile, and not knowing God is the darkest part of that exile. We need to continuously remove ourselves from the Egypt-like dark, exiled situations we create in our lives and come out to embrace God.

Leviticus

Leviticus translates to "And He Called" in Latin. The Hebrew word for it is Vayiqra, sometimes spelled Wayiqra. Throughout Leviticus, the Israelites who were freed from Egypt by Moses on God's command were camped at Mount Sinai. God kept calling Moses to the Tent of Meeting or the Tabernacle to give him further instructions, rules, and laws for His people to abide by. The laws in the Leviticus are highly detailed and were directly given by God Himself.

Also, Moses' brother Aaron and his sons are anointed as Israel's priests. During the anointing ceremony, God appeared in the form of a burst of flame over which the worshippers rejoiced. Leviticus also describes punitive measures taken by God on those who did not follow His commands. He consumed two of Aaron's sons for not preparing correctly before approaching the altar.

The Book of Leviticus has rules for all kinds of human behavior, including the right sexual behavior and what kind of meat should be eaten. It also explains the various ways a person can be considered unclean. Any unclean person had to cleanse himself, undergo penance, and genuinely repent for their actions before they were allowed into the camp again.

Finally, God promised all the people of Israel He would fill the Holy Land with abundance and limitless love if they obeyed all His laws and commandments. Absent obedience, God warned of unpleasant outcomes and hatred from Him. Before you decide that God in Kabbalah is cruel, you must know about a specific annual ritual called the Day of Atonement.

According to Leviticus, the Day of Atonement empowers priests to offer sacrifices as a way of asking for forgiveness from God on behalf of the entire nation. This law is clear evidence of the generosity of God. He decreed that when His followers confessed and repented for their sins in all sincerity, then they could earn back His graces and love.

The Zohar describes the act of a repentant sinner as follows. *"Anyone who has transgressed His commandment, if such a person confesses and offers to rectify himself, then he needs to feel true remorse and sense of brokenness. If he weeps while bringing the sacrifice to God to repent for his sins, then that is better than anything else he does."*

And the priests could do the task of singing God's praises if the sinner who came for repentance was truly broken and remorseful. The priest, as ordained by God, was rooted in kindness and compassion. Priests must always present a smiling and shining face and be happier than the other people because the crown they received from Him when they were anointed empowers them to be so.

Bamidbar - Numbers

At the start of Bamidbar or Numbers, the Israelites prepared to leave Mount Sinai and go toward the Promised Land. God appointed one of the 12 Israeli tribes to help Aaron and his sons in their priestly tasks, including conducting prayers and rituals and maintaining and taking care of all religious items and articles. The tribe God chose was the Levite tribe.

Before they left, the Israelites dedicated the Tabernacle that held the Ark of the Covenant. Clouds that rested over the Tabernacle guided the way for the Israelites. As they entered the desert, the people complained about everything from the smallest to the biggest thing. They found fault with the food served to them and also with the leadership of Moses.

Moses sent many of his men as spies, including Joshua and Caleb, to explore and bring back important information about Canaan so they could prepare to annex it for themselves. Joshua and Caleb returned and said that it was possible to overcome the Canaanites with God's help.

Other spies argued that it was impossible with or without God's help to overcome and conquer Canaan. These spies raised a revolt among the Israelites, telling everyone that the best option was to go back to Egypt. God would get angry at the lack of faith among His people and wanted to destroy them.

Moses pleaded to God on behalf of his people and begged for forgiveness. God agreed to forgive but cursed the Israelites, saying that the present generation, except for Joshua and Caleb, could not enter the Promised Land. So, Moses led his people to wander the wilderness near the Red Sea for forty years.

A second revolt took place when many men became jealous of Moses' popularity and leadership. Again, God got angry at the behavior of the Israelites and wanted to destroy them all. Moses again intervened and begged God to punish only the guilty parties and not the entire nation. Moses tried to warn his people they would die at the hands of God because of their disobedience and lack of faith, but they didn't heed his warning.

God opened up the ground, and all the guilty men were swallowed into the earth. Instead of learning from the mistakes of the dead men, the remaining Israelites blamed Moses and Aaron for the incident. God then sent a fast-spreading plague through the crowd to kill them all, but Aaron held up the priest's censer and stopped the plague from destroying the Israelites.

After this, another incident took place in which both Aaron and Moses disobeyed God's command. The people complained about the lack of water. God ordered Moses to speak to a rock so it would spout water for the people. Instead of speaking to it, Moses struck it with his staff. While water came out of the rock, God got angry at Moses and

Aaron for the brash act. He cursed that neither Moses nor Aaron would be allowed into the Promised Land. Aaron died soon after this incident, and his son, Eleazar, took over the duties of the priesthood.

The people of Israel traveled from place to place throughout little kingdoms in the southwestern parts of Canaan, begging for safe passage through, but they were met with hostility everywhere. Finally, God helped the Israelites defeat the Amorites and settle in their land.

When the King of Moab heard of the overthrow of the Amorites, he sent for a renowned sorcerer named Balaam and ordered him to curse the Israelites before he marched with his soldiers to defeat them. God sent his angel to warn the sorcerer and order him not to curse the Israelites. Balaam agreed, and when the King of Moab arrived, he delivered prophecies proclaiming victory to the people of Israel and death and destruction to Moab.

The Israelites again blundered when the men succumbed to the charms of the native women and worshipped their pagan gods. This time, God sent a devastating plague, and only the sacrifice of an Israeli man with his native mistress would please God, and He ended the plague. This sacrifice was carried out by Eleazar's son, who was now the priest. The forty-year wandering period drew to a close, and Joshua was chosen by God to lead the people.

Devarim - Deuteronomy

The last of the Five Books of Moses, Deuteronomy, began in the fortieth year of the Israelites' wanderings. The new generation which would be allowed to enter the Promised Land was ready, and Moses addressed them before they undertook the holy journey. In his address, Moses summarized everything that took place in the last 40 years. He told the youngsters the importance of remembering and thanking God for his miracles and of His deep connection with the Israelites. He also repeated the ten commandments he received from God at Mount Sinai.

He got all the native inhabitants and symbols of Canaan's pagan gods destroyed so the Israelites could pray to their God with no form of interference. Moses also reinstated several laws and commandments in Leviticus in addition to adding a few new rules such as, *"The Israelis are mandated to cancel all debts every seven years."*

Moses emphasized God's love for Israel and its people. He recalled God's love for oppressed people, widows, and orphans. Israel could do nothing but love God intensely in return and with deep devotion. Moses also told his people to remember and obey God's words. He instructed them to write God's words in their homes and on their bodies. Moses repeatedly stressed the importance of loving God and that commitment to His laws would bring a lot of good for Israel.

Moses also predicted that Israel would lose God's grace because the people would become disobedient. When they repented truly and with deep remorse, then God would accept them back with love.

And finally, as ordered by God, he composed the Song of Moses in which he spoke of the disobedience of the people and praised God's limitless compassion. He said this song would be a constant reminder about God's covenant toward Israel. The song is written in the Book of Laws, which is kept with the Ark of the Covenant. At last, Moses climbed a mountain from where God revealed the Promised Land to him, after which he died. God Himself buried Moses. Moses was praised as the only prophet who performed amazing miracles and knew and met God face-to-face.

In summary, Leviticus, Bamidbar, and Deuteronomy form the bulk of the Torah or Kabbalah Law. Multiple narrations, voices, and actions are used to convey legal matters, procedures, and instructions. These three books documented a crucial period in Israel's history when it was on the path to development with a separate national identity for itself and its people.

The wanderings in the wilderness can be seen as a metaphor for a young nation trying to come to terms with its needs and desires and its powers. It can be seen as a period of learning for the Israelites. Punishments such as exiles for certain errors and crimes reflect the people's desire to remain united as a community following their laws and rules strictly.

Also, Moses extolling God's compassion despite the numerous times when He demonstrated His wrath through famine and disease may be perplexing to new initiates. The divine punitive measures were designed to bring people closer to God and challenge the limits of their faith and conviction in God.

Parables from the Zohar

The Zohar has a veritable collection of parables and stories used to discuss and teach the Torah. Let us look at a couple of them here to help you understand Zohar's context in Kabbalah.

Before we can do that, it is vital that you understand the parables and stories in Zohar go a long way beyond being simple stories. Rabbi Simeon said, "*Fie on those people who think that the Torah is just a collection of simple stories and tales to give us instructions of life. If this was true, then the common people would be able to create a new "Torah" out of simple tales. If the Torah was only to give a background and history of the world, then the ministers and governments would be able to write a new "Torah." Every word in the Torah reflects deep secrets and high wisdom.*"

The tales and narratives in the Torah are mere outer coverings. Anyone who doesn't look beyond the outward covering is spiritually backward. We must delve deeper than the outer layer to understand Torah's true essence. Each parable/story/tale has a deeper underlying meaning that every student must work at unraveling. Often, there are multiple levels of underlying meanings and interpretations in each parable.

Creation of God Parable - This parable in the Zohar describes the first instant of the Creation of the Universe. According to the story, a spark of "impenetrable darkness" flashed within God (or Ein Sof, as God is referred to in the Zohar) just a moment God created the cosmos. At this instant, a ring of vapor and several colors formed around that magical spark.

Then, two things happened simultaneously. Ein Sof "split" and "did not split," which caused a single sliver of light to shine. Zohar explains this moment is the start of the cosmos. The simultaneous "splitting" and "not splitting" of Ein Sof represents the crux of Kabbalah's idea of God, a force that simultaneously and contradictorily exists everywhere (splitting) and exists nowhere (not splitting).

The flash of light sparked by Ein Sof from nothing was so bright that it was like "impenetrable darkness." This concept of "light being so bright that it was visible" is the start of the central paradoxical theme right through the Zohar and Kabbalah. God is so bright that He can be seen. God is everywhere and nowhere.

The first spark that Ein Sof flashed is considered the infinite source of all energy in the entire cosmos. That source of energy powers God Himself and Kabbalah. The ring of various colors that formed around the spark was considered the first sefirah, namely Keter or Divine Crown. The colors represented the remaining nine sefirot. This topic is taken up later on in the book.

The Zohar, through this parable, re-instills the belief that the cosmos was created out of nothingness. Kabbalah thrives on the mysteries and unknowability in the cosmos. That several questions remain unanswered (at least logically speaking) is not a matter of concern for Kabbalists. Using this parable reflects the love for mysticism in Kabbalah. Kabbalists do not dismiss what they don't understand. They strive to learn and unravel one layer at a time until they understand.

The Essence of Torah Parable - There was once a man who lived in the mountains. He grew wheat and ate it raw. This man visited the city one day and tasted bread for the first time. He loved it. Then he ate a piece of cake and enjoyed its taste even more than bread. Then he went on to eat pastries, and their delicious taste delighted the mountain man.

Finally, someone told him that the bread, cake, and pastries were all made from wheat. Now, he gloated to everyone in the city he was the "master of pastries, cakes, and bread" because he consumed the raw essence (wheat) of the three delicious dishes.

This parable in the Zohar has a deep meaning. Wheat, bread, cake, and pastry symbolize four layers or levels of knowledge in the Torah. Wheat is the simplest level wherein the student knows the laws and the stories of the Torah. The other elements, namely bread, cake, and pastry, represent higher stages of learning:

- Bread stands for the understanding of the homilies and the morals they teach.

- The cake represents the allegorical and spiritual understanding of the Torah's teachings.

- The pastry is the highest level of understanding, namely the mystical truths in the stories and teachings of the Torah. At the pastry level, a student feels a close connection to God.

The vain mountain man believed that he knew everything there was to be known and that he was a master because he had eaten the raw essence. He believed that by eating raw wheat, he understood the other delicious products that could be made with wheat. But, through this parable, Zohar teaches us that the man was mistaken, and we should be careful not to be mistaken as he was.

Understanding the essence of the Torah is gradual and difficult. It cannot be learned and mastered instantly. The Zohar tells us we can master the Torah only through deep meditation, extensive study, and religiously reading and rereading the texts.

The Parable of the Old Man and the Ravishing Maiden - As explained in the earlier chapters, the Zohar involves discussions among the companions of Rabbi Simeon about the Torah. Also, they discussed the Torah in various ways. Sometimes, the characters were discussed. Sometimes, the companions themselves become characters for a better understanding of God's Word.

In this parable, Rabbi Yose and Rabbi Hiyya met at the Tower of Tyre. Rabbi Yose complained to Rabbi Hiyya about an old donkey driver who pestered him with difficult riddles. When Rabbi Hiyya listened to the riddles that the donkey driver had asked Rabbi Jose, the former realizes that the old donkey driver was actually a very wise man. They both set out to find the donkey driver.

They found the old man and sat with him talking. The old man told them a story of a ravishing maiden. This maiden lived hidden deep in a beautiful palace. She had one lover who passed the gates of the palace every day to get a glimpse of her. She and her lover had never had a face-to-face meeting. The maiden loved her lover very much, and out of this love, she showed her face at a window for a short while. Almost immediately, she withdrew from the window.

The wise old donkey driver compared the maiden to the Torah. The beautiful maiden tempted her lover with one look and quickly withdrew. The two rabbis were astonished by the power of this parable and realized the depth of wisdom of the old man. The donkey driver then revealed his true identity to the two Rabbis. He was Yeiva Sava, also called Yeiva, the Elder, a famous old wise man of those times.

Through this parable, we learn that the wisdom and knowledge of the Torah can lurk in the unlikeliest of places. Rabbi Yose should have focused more on the intelligence of the riddles asked by the donkey driver to realize he was wise. Instead, Rabbi Yose focused on his shabby appearance and wrote him off as an annoying old man with many incomprehensible riddles.

Only when he sat with Rabbi Hiyya and listened to the old man's words did Rabbi Yose realize his intelligence and wisdom. Until then, he was blinded to the inner wisdom of the man. This lesson of giving respect to the wise is the fundamental concept in Kabbalah. Through this parable, the Zohar teaches us that the things worth learning are shrouded in mysteries and often shabby appearances that need to be unraveled and understood through respectful contemplation.

The story of the ravishing maiden is also a core concept of Kabbalah. The Torah and the Zohar are seen as out-of-reach beautiful maidens who lovers want to conquer and experience. But the maidens seem difficult to conquer. Occasionally, the lovers may see a glimpse of understanding – as a lover gets a glimpse of his maiden.

The flashes of understanding inflame the reader's curiosity to know and understand the Torah better, just as glimpses of the ravishing maiden inflame the lover's desire to meet and unite with her. Another vital Kabbalistic belief comes through from this parable. Just as the lover keeps passing the maiden's gate every day, a loyal student will try to gradually understand the mystical Kabbalah texts by consistently reading and learning every day.

Chapter Five: The Ten Sefirot: God and Creation; Keter, Hokhmah, and Binah

A distinguishing feature of Kabbalah is the theory of the ten sefirot or ten creative forces or ten emanations intertwined in the cosmos and connect the Infinite, God or Ein Sof, and our world. Sefirot is sometimes spelled as sephiroth, and its singular is sefirah.

The ten sefirot find mention in the Sefer Yetzirah, one of the earliest Kabbalistic works. According to a verse in this hallowed Kabbalah text, there are ten numbers, the same as sefirot. There are 22 Hebrew alphabets. The ten numbers and the 22 alphabets are the foundation of everything in the cosmos. Of the 22 alphabets, three are called "mothers," seven of the letters are called "double," and 12 are "simple."

The ten sefirot are the ten vessels of light and water through which God created the world. One of the most mysterious and powerful aspects of the ten sefirot is that each exists separately and together simultaneously. The ten sefirot are of God, and they are also God.

As God's power is infinite, He created the ten sefirot as His extensions to be His messengers so His vast and limitless energy could spread across the limited human world. The sefirot are formless and contain limitless energy. The energy of the ten sefirot reflects the limitless energy of God or Ein Sof.

Yet, the ten sefirot cannot define or limit God. The Kabbalists could identify each character in the stories of the Torah as one configuration of the sefirot. The sefirot function like hypostases, which can be defined as abstract concepts visualized as real beings and being parts of reality but are more real than the physical world we live in.

The Structure of the Sefirot

The Zohar describes the sefirot as an essential aspect of the world. It emanated in the form of a balance scale or Mishkal. Like the balance scale, the structure of the sefirot has a right, left, and center and can be imagined in the form of a triad or triangle. This structure allows each of the sefirah in the sefirot to share creative forces with the others around it.

Kabbalists also portray the sefirot on a Tree of Life, which is like a visual map. The position of each sefirah on the Tree of Life represents several qualities, including its position on God's body, its gender, etc. The ten sefirot are the following

- Keter or the Divine Crown
- Hokhmah or Wisdom
- Binah or Understanding
- Hesed or Mercy
- Din or Justice
- Tiferet or Beauty
- Nezah or Eternity
- Hod or Glory

- Yesod or Foundation

- Shekhinah or the presence of God or Ein Sof in this world

The ten sefirot emerged out of God's body, with Keter being the first one. The right side of the balance, which has Hokhmah, Hesed, and Neah stands for benevolence, harmony, and unity and represents the masculine side. It is connected to the bestowing and blessings of goodness showered upon our world and is embodied in the Sefirah of Hesed.

The left side of the scale or tree of life, which has Binah, Gevurah, and Hod, is the feminine side and stands for strict justice and power. It represents the fearsome awe of God and also the principles of separation and distinction. When the left side, which is embodied in the Sefirah of Din, may dominate in an unrestrained manner, then it gives rise to evil.

The center of the sefirot structure, which has Keter, Tiferet, Yesod, and Shekhinah, and that which are embodied in the Sefirah of Tiferet represents the perfect balance of mercy and divine justice. This exists between the Din and Hesed and the feminine and masculine aspects. The feminine aspects are believed to be the daughters of Binah. Binah is also called the "Mother of the ten sefirot."

The Kabbalah recognizes the importance of balance and is rooted in the belief that the cosmos would not survive if it were based only on divine justice or only on divine mercy. A balanced equation of the two is imperative.

The "balance scale" structure also helps to keep the sefirot intact even when it feels the influx of God's power. Also, each of the ten sefirot contains an element of the other nine within it. This interconnected nature of the sefirot is one of the primary reasons for their divinity and infinity.

The Sefirot and the Creation of the Cosmos

The Kabbalistic Creation Myth starts with the following sentence, "*In the beginning, there was nothing but the Light.*" And then continues in the following way: When there was only "The Light," there was no time, space, or motion. The Light was the first cause. If the Light wanted to give, who or what would it give it, as nothing existed but it did?

And so, it created a vessel that would receive everything the Light offered. The vessel's job was nothing more than to receive what was given to it. The only desire of the vessel was the "Desire to Receive." Kabbalah describes the Light to be the first cause and the vessel to be the first effect. Further, the vessel creation was the only act of creation, and everything that followed was the effects of that one creative act.

So, there was Light, the giver, and there was the vessel, the receiver. Since time and space did not exist, the vessel was being filled up endlessly by the Light, which was the ideal situation; it was paradise. However, soon things changed because the vessel inherited the Desire to Give and Share from the Light, its Creator. The vessel desired to be the cause, which made the vessel feel good. It wanted to give its own, share its own light, and become more of a cause and less of an effect.

There was now a conflict. How could a vessel whose very nature was to receive express its desire to give and share? Giving was not part of its function. So, the vessel did something strange. It stopped receiving from the Light, pushed it back, and said, "Enough, no more!"

The Light said to the vessel, "I understand your desire to be a cause and to share and give and express yourself." Meaning the Light, like a loving parent, stood back and withdrew, allowing the vessel, its child, to take its first tentative steps. The Light gave space for the vessel to share and become the causative force instead of being only the effect.

So, the vessel now had its own sacred space to express its desires of giving and sharing. This space was the cause that created our physical realm. And in this sacred space, the vessel exploded into innumerable pieces. These fragments became matter and energy that resulted in the entire cosmos and its elements, including atoms, humans, people, plants, and everything else.

God's process to create the universe is referred to as "tzimtzum," which translates to "stepping back" in Hebrew. God "took a step back" so that another "Order" or "Else" can come into being so the desires of the vessel could be fulfilled. The Kabbalah concept of free will is also rooted in this idea, which was the starting point of creating the universe.

When God or Ein Sof created life, He essentially subdued the all-encompassing and omnipotent Divine Presence to give place for Divine Will to realize as other beings. According to Kabbalah, this space was given to us by Ein Sof so we could be "human as divinely possible and divine as humanly possible." Therefore, our world is a sacred space where we can err, fall, doubt, believe, laugh, cry, and do everything else as humans. The world was created by Ein Sof, the Limitless and Boundless One, by "stepping back," which translates into an act of humility to honor a separate reality.

The Kabbalah creation myth focuses on three pertinent symbols, namely:

- The "Tzimtzum" or the "self-limiting" aspect of God.
- The "Shevirah" or the breaking of the vessel.
- The "Tikkun" or the harmonious mending and correction of the mistakes brought into this world by the "Shevirah."

Keter

Keter was the first sefirah that emerged from God's body. It lies on top of the tree. Keter translates to the Divine Crown or Supreme Crown. The crown, worn above the head, represents the topmost aspect of the Sefirot that humans can contemplate. Kabbalists rarely discuss this sefirot. Some later works describe Keter as 620 radiating pillars of light.

Keter represents Divine Will, and all pleasure and delight arise from it. It is the source of all the power that can activate the soul. Keter refers to things beyond and above the human mind's capabilities of understanding. The other nine sefirot are described as the physical body that starts from the head and moves downwards into action. The crown lying above the head of a king is connected to the concept of "monarchy," which is an intangible, abstract element above the tangible, concrete king's head.

Keter stands for the primal instincts of the intent of God or Ein Sof. It represents the initial desire of the Light to bring forth elements so it can express its Desire of Giving and Sharing. It is vital to remember here that although Ein Sof contains all the potential for creation, it also has no content, which is why it is called by names such as "The Hidden Light," "Nothing," "That which cannot be grasped."

Keter is the link between God's infinite world and our finite world. In the stages of creation, Keter is considered that point at which the material world we can sense, touch, feel, see, and smell comes into being. Keter also represents the source of sensory experience, and this source is believed to be God's head.

Since Keter represents the desire of Ein Sof to bring the world into being, this sefirah is also about absolute compassion. The name of God connected with Keter is Ehyeh Asher Ehyeh. This is the name He used to show Himself to Moses as a burning bush. The name Ehyeh is the infinite source of all sustenance.

In the balance scale structure of the Sefirot, Keter is placed right on top between Hokhmah (on its right) and Binah (on its left). The Zohar describes Keter as the "most hidden of all hidden things," making it the most sublime of all the sefirot.

Rabbi Moses Cordovero describes Keter as the source of the 13 Supernal Attributes of Mercy, which was given to Moses by God in the Exodus. God told Moses that if Israelis recited these attributes of mercy when pleading for forgiveness, then He would forgive their sins. Keter is colorless and invisible.

A deeper understanding of Keter - Interestingly, sometimes, Keter is not counted among the ten sefirot, and Da'at replaces Keter. When Keter is included, then Da'at is absent in the list of ten. When Keter is absent, then the sefirot is portrayed as a chain of command, beginning with Hokhmah or the intellect and ending with the implementation represented by Shekhinah or Malchut.

Keter is one step ahead of the Hokhmah because the idea or the intellect is really not the beginning of an implementation. The true start is the existence of "desire" or "will." Let us take a simple analogy to understand the position of Keter when it is above the ten sefirot.

If someone wants to build a home, typically, the image or idea of their future home is the start of the entire process until the actual home is built. The real beginning of the journey of building a home is not the idea or the image of the home but the "desire" or "will" to build it. This desire is analogous to Keter.

Keter is not always included as part of the ten sefirot because desire or will is such a deep trait and such a fundamental aspect of life it is not easily quantifiable. In the above example, you can trace the individual's reason or motivation to build their house up to a certain level only.

He or she wants to build his house to show off. Why does he want to show off? Because he or she wants to feel good. Why? Because it feels important to feel good. Why? Because that's what he or she wants? You cannot go beyond a certain point when you hit the desire or will button, and after that, there is nothing else. This desire can't be analyzed by our limited cause-effect metrics. This desire is what Keter is all about.

In higher spiritual realms, Keter is God's primary will or the ultimate Divine Will and is beyond analysis and purview of metrics and measuring tools. The other sefirot are divine tools but quantifiable through an interlocking chain of cause and effect. Because Keter is only a cause, it cannot be part of the sefirot system.

The only point we can reach regarding the root of the ultimate Divine will is that "He wants to bestow good on His entire Creation and creatures." We cannot find an answer to the next logical question, "Why does God want to do that?" Such a question may not be a valid one when we deal with higher levels of spirituality. Therefore, Keter does not have a cause we humans can yet relate to. The effects of Keter work similarly. There are two effects, namely:

- Direct, mechanical effects - this type is easy to understand. You flick a switch, which results in two pieces of metal connecting with each other, and the light comes on.

- Indirect, diffusing effects - this effect is mostly felt through writings and teachings that stir up and change people.

Indirect, diffusing effects cannot be quantified or observed directly. Keter's effects are of the second type wherein it affects all the other sefirot but not in any quantifiable or discernible way. The first group of sefirot (if you don't include Keter) are Hokhmah, Binah, and Da'at. These three sefirot are rooted in rationality, and their direct causes and effects are organizable and quantifiable.

Anything that precedes these sefirot are outside rationality as it cannot be structured or quantified. Therefore, while there is no doubt that the sefirah of Keter is the source of other sefirot following it, there is no way of telling when, where, and how much it affects the creative progressive.

The other sefirot are comparable to the body, starting from the head and moving downward. Keter, on the other hand, translates to "crown," which lies above the head. As mentioned earlier, the crown is related to "monarchy," an abstract, intangible, and unquantifiable element that lies on the head of a king.

Keter is not like mechanical elements of the body like the head, arms, legs, etc., and not even like the more subtle like the mind and intellect. Keter is something that is beyond this and "endows" royalty on the person who wears it. And this is why Keter is sometimes a sefirah, and other times, not a sefirah. It exists and is the source of all sefirot and yet cannot be counted along with them.

One quote in Kabbalah is, *"And Hokhmah comes from nowhere and nothing,"* specifically when seen as the first sefirah. This "nothing" and "nowhere" is actually Keter.

Hokhmah or Wisdom

Also called Chochmah, this sefirah arises from Keter and represents wisdom. In the stages of creation, Hokhmah stands for the origin of mental energy and thought. It stands for intuitive power and intuitive knowledge.

This sefirah channelizes the pure energy of Keter into a kind that can form the intellect and the mind. Located on the right side of the Tree of Life, Hokhmah is of masculine gender and is associated with force. It is believed to represent the right hemisphere of God's brain.

Out of the ten sefirot, Hokhmah or Chochmah or wisdom is a powerful divine emanation with the power to create "something out of nothing," because, as we have seen earlier that it truly comes from Keter, which is not quantifiable or measurable in any human way.

Hokhmah is the wisdom put into the mind. It is the flash of inspiration and the information we have learned. When an idea pops in our heads, this is Hokhmah. Chochmah, the other word for Hokhmah, comes from two Hebrew words, namely "koach" and "mah," which translates to "potential." Therefore, this sefirah is pure divine potential or an idea emanating from divine will or desire. This idea is waiting to be developed.

It might be a good idea to explain this concept of "creating something from nothing" by comparing editing and writing tasks. What do editors do? They look at a piece of writing, look at the words, phrases, and sentences used to make sure they are presented so it conveys the desired meaning to readers. Editing has a structure of format that can be explained to students.

Now, suppose the writer of this piece was asked this question. "How did you get this creative idea?" He or she might tell the students of an incident that triggered a certain or something else that gave him or her the idea for the creative piece. The writer might explain the various ways you can stimulate your brain to think differently and form ideas and patterns. However, "creativity" by itself does not have a logical structure. An idea has to be already in place for logical processing to start.

Therefore, creating something comes literally from nowhere and is called the "ex-nihilo" process. So, Hokhmah follows nothing but is simply a moment of inspiration that emerges from nowhere and from nothing. When this inspiration emerges, it gets logically fleshed out in ways that can be understood and ready for subsequent action.

This is why Kabbalists strongly believe that wisdom is not only difficult to find but also "nowhere" specific to be found. Further, it is not possible to inquire and find answers intellectually above the level of Hokhmah. Kabbalah says that we can research, enquire, analyze, and think about God's work and activities only up to a certain point. Beyond this point, it is impossible to connect with the divine merely through intelligence because God's providence does not flow through this channel.

Binah or Understanding

Binah is the first sefirah on the left side of the Tree of Life, the side that stands for structure, justice, and femininity. In the stages of creation, Binah follows Hokhmah evolving from pure intellectual energy to form thoughts and ideas. It represents the synthetic and analytical power of the mind.

Binah is considered the first female energy and receives the seeds of Hokhmah to conceive the lower seven sefirot. Representing the left side of God's brain, Binah is believed to be the mother of all the ten sefirot and the source of all creating beings. Binah is the womb in which raw understanding is processed and developed.

Binah represents "processed wisdom" or deductive reasoning. It is the power to distinguish one idea from another. When Hokhmah generates an idea, it remains unproductive and raw if it is left that way. An idea by itself is not useful. However, when we analyze the ideas, understand their parameters and axioms, think about the implications of the ideas and their consistencies and inconsistencies when the rawness slowly disappears, and the idea gets to the processing mode.

Kabbalists use a father and mother metaphor to describe the relationship between an unprocessed idea and a processed one. The Hokhmah sefirah is a little seed that a father sows. It is infinitesimally small and contains an undeveloped potential to become something. When this seed sown by the father gets into the mother's womb, then it develops into a baby, which can be likened to the processed idea.

Here's another metaphor found in Talmudic literature that is related to the connection of a father and mother needed to bring about action. The man brings wheat from the fields and wool from the sheep. These two items represent potential or unprocessed ideas. Then, the woman of the house has the power to convert the wheat and wool into flour for food and clothes to wear. Binah is that mother who develops the potential in every idea in the Hokhnah sefirah.

The study of the Torah can also be used to understand the contrast between Hokhnah and Binah. Let us try and understand this in a bit of detail. God gave Moses the Torah to be passed on to the Israelites. In addition, God gave Moses the art of pilpul, too, which helped Moses to logically extrapolate the existing body of law to form new laws of the Torah.

Moses was not mandated to hand over the art of pilpul to anyone else. However, from the goodness of his heart, he passed on the skill to other Israelites. After Moses died, this was useful for Israel because the people forgot many laws. These forgotten laws were restored through the art of pilpul left behind by Moses.

This Talmudic lesson describes the roles of Hokhmah and Binah in the study of the Torah. Torah is an example of Hokhmah because it represents God's wisdom injected into our world. The validity of the Torah doesn't come from our understanding but because it is God's word. Torah has an inbuilt Binah because if we know the basics, we can use logical extrapolation to rebuild and develop it.

Kabbalistic method of studying the Torah might seem strange to most of the new entrants. While students have a huge reverence for the Torah because it is God's word, they also debate every point using the keenest logic possible. This is the power of the combination of Hokhmah and Binah elements. Torah contains the divinity bestowed from God and the Binah through the art of pilpul developing and expanding it.

To summarize, Hokhmah is the intellect that does not use a rational process to emerge. It is inspired rather than taught in any structured, orderly manner. On the other hand, Binah is based on rationality and has the power to develop the smallest seed of an idea through to its full potential.

Chapter Six: Hesed, Gevurah, and Tiferet

Hesed or Mercy

The sefirot before Hesed or Chesed are all attributes of the intellect and come before the stage of implementation. The sefirot after this are attributes of "action," and the first "action" is Hesed, which translates to kindness.

Hesed is the fourth sefirah and the first child of Binah. Also called Chesed, this sefirah stands for mercy and love. Hesed represents the irrepressible urge to expand. Lying on the right side of the Mishkal or the balance scale (or the Tree of Life), Hesed is masculine energy and is associated with force. In the process of creation, Hesed represents the start of emotional energy.

The fourth sefirah tempers Hokhmah's pure intellectual energy with mercy and love. Hesed represents God's right arm and is considered the brother of Din or Gevurah, the sefirah representing God's left arm. Gevurah and Hesed are at opposing poles of God's identity.

While Hesed represents unconditional love and mercy, Din or Gevurah represents control and limitation. The fourth and fifth sefirot, namely Hesed and Din, function together in the same way Binah and Hokhmah balance and modify each other's traits. Kabbalists identify Hesed with Abraham, the patriarch of the Israelites.

Mercy, compassion, and kindness are normally synonymous with niceness. However, the meaning of Chesed goes deeper than this usual meaning. In Kabbalah, Chesed is considered an act that has no "cause." It stands alone and unconditional. Therefore, the fourth sefirah, Chesed, is above all other sefirot because it is unmotivated and unconditional.

Let us try and explain this a little better. When you work for somebody, you get paid. The payment is nothing more than recycling your own action. For example, if you work in a corporate house, then the energy you spend on working for the company gets recycled back to you in the form of a salary, which you use to buy food and create more energy to work, get paid, buy more, create energy, and so forth. The cycle continues endlessly. And this is true for any work you do.

An act of chesed is, on the other hand, not recycled. It works like an anonymous donation set up for a scholarship fund. Also, chesed is a proactive sefirah. It states any interaction, which is the reason it is the first sefirah of action. Being the first "action," sefirah means Hesed contains a unique property that does not exist in any other element of the universe.

Every action in the cosmos has a cause, except the first one. In the sphere of action, Hesed is the first action without a cause, and this unique property expresses its expansiveness. Creation is an action of Chesed, not only because creation came from nothing (or is an ex-nihilo process), but it also refers to the interaction between humans and God.

Many of us have the wrong notion that since the world and cosmos are already in place, its continuation depends entirely on human work and effort. We believe that we are rewarded with the world when we fulfill God's commandments. Nothing is further from the truth, according to Kabbalah. Creation was a unilateral act, and there is nothing "deserving" about receiving the cosmos from God. Therefore, creation is Chesed.

Our relationship with God is built on the foundation of Chesed. Sadly, many of us who don't understand this concept end up "blaming" God He has not done enough for us. We fight with Him and argue that He has done injustices to us. Therefore, when we call upon God to do something for us, our prayers are based on the idea that "He owes us something."

We use the argument we would use with our employer that "We should be paid our dues for the work we did." However, this cannot work with God. We cannot litigate with God because, in the God-man relationship, we are the alms collector, and He is the donor.

To take an example, if an injustice happens to us, we cannot go to God and say, "Why are You doing this to me? I don't deserve this suffering." This kind of fight with God for what you deserve is not the Chesed way because no one or nothing in this cosmos "deserves" to be born or merited their own existence. The basic foundation of this premise in Kabbalah is that existence and creation are gifts from God, and therefore, while we can question God's actions, we cannot debate or litigate with Him.

The concept of Chesed is to be used in every mitzvah, too, according to Kabbalists. The purity of your motive is a critical aspect of the Hesed sefirah. If motivation is based on a pay-off of any kind, including fame, money, success, popularity, or anything else, then the Hesed sefirah is absent in that mitzvah. The slightest hint of expectation of any return takes away the purity of the Chesed in action. That action becomes just another link to the long, limitless chain of cause and effects.

The Hesed sefirah is also the reason parents are accorded a special status in our lives. Frequently, the honoring of our parents is believed to be an act of gratitude to them for having given birth to us and all the other favors bestowed on us. However, Hesed sefirah goes deeper than this.

Hesed explains that our parents giving us the gift of existence is the only pure Chesed they do for us. The same goes for our children. The only chesed act we do is give our children the gift of life, unconditionally and with no expectations. Any other favors that parents do for children belong to a dimension lower than pure Chesed. The gift of life is the only Chesed act and, Kabbalah teaches us to give our parents the same respect and love we give God.

To summarize, Chesed or Hesed is the first step of action not preceded by any deed. Chesed, like the process of creation, is ex-nihilo, and comes from nothing, and is unconditional. Chesed is the first sefirah that describes the start of the God-human relationship.

Din, Gevurah, or Justice

Gevurah is the second sefirah of action and brings strict justice into the cosmos. Gevurah translates to "judgment" or "strength." It is a feminine sefirah located on the left side of the Tree of Life. Gevurah represents emotional energy, just as Hesed does. The difference between Hesed and Din sefirot is that the latter uses judgment. Restraint and strict justice, whereas the former uses mercy and love.

Gevurah is the inward withdrawal of forces. It is the source of fear, hatred, terror, justice, control, and restraint. Like opposing forces, Din and Hesed balance each other to preserve order in the cosmos. Gevurah is associated with Isaac, son of Abraham and father of Jacob. Gevurah or "strength" represents God's fury and power of absolute judgment.

This sefirah is usually understood as God's way of judging humans and punishing the wrongdoers and the wicked. Gevurah is founded on absolute adherence to the word of law and following it stringently. Gevurah is all about meting out justice in the cosmos. It is clear that Din or Gevurah is in complete contract with Mercy and Chesed, based on unconditional compassion. Therefore, the sefirot teaches us that God's primary action modes are kindness of Chesed versus strictness, justice, and stringency of Gevurah.

While the above understanding is not completely wrong, the concept of the fifth sefirah goes deeper, just like Chesed goes beyond mere kindness as we humans know and experience. Again, understanding the Creation act, which needed limitless Chesed, will help us delve deeper into the idea of Gevurah.

God said, "Let there be a firmament." On this command based on the limitless Chesed of God, the cosmos expanded and stretched and continued to do so until God again commanded, "Enough." At this command, the expansion of the world came to a standstill.

From this, we can understand that Chesed by itself is limitless and unbounded. When He said "enough," His beneficence remained boundless, but the gifts He bestowed were limited by human limitation. "Measure for measure" is based on what each of us deserves and merits, which is limited and clearly defined. Gevurah limits Chesed just as the amount of money we have limits what we can buy.

In this context, we have to recall the important boundless act of Chesed. When something is given in Chesed mode, then there is no limit and boundaries. While humans are limited by resources and multiple other things in our limited world, God's Chesed is boundless.

The command in the act of creation, which says "enough," introduced a new concept into the human world, that of limitations, boundaries, and the idea of "finiteness." This definition of limitation and boundary is not based on the limit of God's resources because that aspect is unlimited. The limitation is because of the receiver's limitations. God decides that He will give something for something.

Therefore, if a person has sufficient purchasing power, they can gain a lot from God.

The system of reward and punishment in the human world is rooted in the Gevurah sefirah. So, the obvious question is, "Why did God limit kindness? Why did He not bestow His infinite Chesed on us?" The answer to this question is that if God gave us His infinite bounty, then our existence would have no meaning. Everything that lived, including us, would result from His generosity. Whether humans existed or not, the world will always receive His bounties. Instead, if our world was filled with what we have earned and merited, then our lives would be meaningful.

Here is a great analogy to explain the concept of meaningfulness and its importance in our lives. Suppose you were hired to do the job of making clay pots in a factory. Let us assume you were paid a certain amount as salary. Now, one day, for some reason, you come to the factory late at night when all the workers have gone home, and you see that all the pots you made during the day were destroyed and turned into clay again. Then, you realize that your payment was nothing more than charity. Would you like to continue working in this factory despite knowing your work is meaningless?

The same thing happens with a person that is bedridden. They might have the money and caregivers to look after their physical needs, but they are bound to shrivel up both emotionally and mentally. The individual's existence loses its value because a person's life is not just dependent on the goodness of other people but their own actions and behaviors that render them an individual.

You can see a huge paradox in this concept. On the one hand, we are awed by Gevurah, knowing its power. We also know how our actions and behaviors are scrutinized to ensure justice is rendered. But we must also survive by the strength of our actions and behaviors. This paradox creates struggle in our lives, undoubtedly. And yet, that is the only way we can live.

If we lived by the boundlessness of Chesed, then our lives would be similar to a mentally ill or physically handicapped person whose life is dependent completely on the goodwill and largesse of others. Such people might not lack food, clothing, or basic shelter, but they can never actualize their lives fully, making them meaningless and worthless.

Gevurah works as a restraining order and is an essential aspect of our world. This statement seems in contrast to the previous sefirah, namely Chesed, where we said that Creation is an act of Chesed. So, why would Gevurah be created in a world brought into being by God's unconditional mercy and compassion? Remember that we must not confuse the act of Creation with the modus operandi of life as willed by God.

For example, let us look at the answer to the question, "What is a wise way of raising a child?" All good-intending parents would want their children to stand and live independently on their own merit and strength. Parents educate so that children learn lessons that will provide the means of independent sustenance.

Here, the initial act of giving life to their children was Chesed, which was preceded by nothing else or was not done in anticipation of future payoffs. The initial Chesed sparked the existence of the child. However, the next part involved Gevurah, where restraint played an important role in helping their children lead a meaningful life independently. In the same way, creation was an act of Chesed, but ongoing God-man relationships and the continued existence of humans was based on Gevurah or strict justice.

Another misleading element needs to be corrected. Gevurah, at first glance, might refer to God's fury to punish wicked people, an act that might seem like a mighty conquest. However, the basic aspect of Gevurah is restraint or to hold back the good that would have been bestowed upon humans had they followed God's word strictly. Therefore, Gevurah is an act of restraint and constraint more than conquering or punishing evil.

Kabbalah teaches us that a strong person can sublimate his own passions and desires. What is the meaning of this lesson? The first lesson is that our power to withstand and overcome an internal urge should be greater than the power needed to oppose an external force. The second lesson is that restraining a primary urge consistently requires far more power than doing one act of greatness.

To reiterate, Chesed is the primal force in the cosmos and is a manifestation of the Divine to bestow upon the human world His limitless mercy and bounties. Gevurah is the second force that restrains the first force and holds back God from giving everything. The strength to restrain is more difficult to achieve than the strength to give.

Here is a classic analogy to explain the relationship between God and humans based on Chesed and Gevurah. Suppose a parent is watching his toddler trying to walk. The toddler is likely to fall repeatedly before he can walk on his own. Until then, the parent needs to muster every ounce of strength to restrain himself from extending a helping hand to his toddler. This restraining power is what Gevurah is all about.

Tiferet or Beauty

Tiferet is the sixth sefirah, which represents beauty and compassion. Tiferet is the balanced combination of Hesed's mercy and Din's strict judgment. Lying in the center of the Tree of Life, Tiferet emanates from God's chest. According to Kabbalistic beliefs, judgment without compassion and mercy is the root of all evil, and it terms such a condition as Sitra Aha or "the other side."

Evil comes forth in the universe only when Tiferet fails to balance Hesed's mercy and Gevurah's judgment. Tiferet is associated with Jacob, the son of Isaac. Tiferet is considered the center of the ten sefirot because it balances and mediates between Chesed and Gevurah. The literal translation of the word "Tiferet" is "middle" and denotes a sense of compromise. However, in the ten sefirot context,

Tiferet has a far more positive connotation than mere compromise. While Tiferet uses a little of Chesed and a little of Gevurah, the usage is dynamic. The amount of each of these previous two sefirot used is different for different modes of activity.

Let us take an example to understand this concept. A defense lawyer's job is to protect his or her client, regardless of innocence or guilt. A prosecutor's job is to prosecute the alleged accused, regardless of innocence or guilt. Each of these two people works from an opposing viewpoint, and it is their task to do so. They cannot take each other's stand and dilute their own perspective of the case.

The judge and jury's task is to look at both sides of the argument and decide on the case and deliver the best outcome. The judge and jury have a higher station and must consider the merits and demerits of both sides, look into the values, goals, and principles of the justice system and take appropriate calls for each case presented to them by the two opposing parties.

Here is another interesting analogy to demonstrate the function of the Tiferet sefirah. Every country in this world is trying its best to survive and provide its citizens the best possible life. There are two departments with seemingly opposing viewpoints. One department is usually called the "state department" (some nations call it the "Foreign Affairs" department), and the second is the defense department.

Every country's defense department looks at every nation as a potential enemy regardless of the diplomatic ties that might exist between the two nations. They work on the belief that warring is an instinct element in humans and all nations, even the friendly ones, are enemies of their state. Therefore, the defense department continuously prepares the nation for war by building and developing defense systems to maintain stability and strength.

On the other hand, the state department works on the premise that humans are inherently peace-loving, and the first option should always be to maintain a friendly and understanding relationship with other nations. The state department focuses on building economic and cultural exchange with other countries of the world, believing the concessions and compromises are good for the stability of the country.

Each of these two departments is mandated to focus on its own viewpoint and use that as the premise to do their assigned tasks. However, someone sitting at a higher station like the head of that nation takes a call at each stage and chooses the state department's or the defense department's strategy depending on a multitude of factors. This person or persons sitting at a higher station has an inner and better worldview of the nation's path, including goals and philosophies based on which different decisions emerge in different situations.

For example, in one case, a friendly (Chesed) approach would be better, while in another, an offensive (Gevurah) approach might be a better option. This decision is based on the ideology of each of the two departments but from the person or persons sitting in the higher station and based on an all-encompassing ideology that works best for the nation as a whole. Tiferet works similarly, taking into account the elements of Chesed and Gevurah, and the outcomes can vary depending on each situation.

Chesed is rooted in mercy and goodness, and its inherent quality is to give for the sake of giving and has no other motive or expectation. The ultimate goal of Chesed is boundless mercy. Contrarily. Gevurah works on restraint and is rooted in the ideology of "quid pro quo," which means everything has to be earned, and nothing comes free. The ultimate goal of Gevurah is to see that every creature earns its way in its life.

Now, Tiferet creates a synthesis of these two opposing viewpoints and considers both approaches to serve the broader and bigger purpose. Tiferet's ultimate goal is the development of humans to their highest potential. For this to happen, sometimes, people may earn their merits, while at other times, some people are given free, unearned bounty.

It is vital to remember that the philosophy of "absolutely no free lunches" or "getting freebies boundlessly" is not valid. Each element could be used to achieve the higher purpose of life, and this approach belongs to Tiferet. Again, the analogy of the parent-child relationship comes in handy to understand this perspective.

Healthy parenthood's ultimate aim is to ensure children develop the best way they can to achieve self-actualization. The child may use their own capabilities, so he or she can improve at every stage of growth. However, when the child has failed despite all their efforts, a "free lunch" needs to be provided to keep the motivation high and push them to continue working towards their goals despite their failures.

Therefore, Tiferet is not a "compromise," which has a more demeaning connotation considering that often it calls for overriding one's vision of integrity. Tiferet is the act of removing the more dangerous element of the two, so progress happens, and mutual destruction is avoided. Tiferet is an essential part of the process because Chesed and Gevurah work in an implacably interlocked manner.

Tiferet unifies the powers of Chesed and Gevurah to prevent combat and achieve the best outcome in any situation. This is the reason "Tiferet," which means beauty gets its name. Beauty is an element of human life whose goal is to integrate elements and combine them to get optimal outcomes. When black and white are combined, you get beauty. Beauty does not mean turning everything into gray by combining black and white. It is the way of combining black and white, so a deep, meaningful picture emerges from the combination.

Chapter Seven: Netzach, Hod, Yesod, and Malchut

Netzach or Eternity and Hod or Glory

Netzach, also called Nezah, is the seventh sefirah and stands for eternity, endurance, or victory. However, the most common representation of Nezah is God's limitless mercy. On the right side of the Tree of Life, Nezah is of masculine gender and represents God's right leg. The seventh sefirah is associated with Moses, the man who led the Israelites out of Egypt to the Promised Land as ordered by God.

The last three sefirot, namely Hod, Yesod, and Shekhinah, are closely linked with the physical world of humans. In Kabbalah, this world is called "material reality." Hod represents the sensory world, including sights, sounds, smells, etc. While Nezah is more undefined spiritual energy, Hod tempers it with some form just as Gevurah tempers Chesed's mercy with judgment. Hod is often associated with Aaron, brother of Moses and the first high priest of the Israelites. The eighth sefirah represents God's left leg.

Netzach and Hod are "tactical" sefirot because their purpose is not inherent in these two but is used for other things. For example, a parent who loves his child immeasurably wants the best for the child. So, it is possible that often this parent uses strict disciplinary actions to drive the child to be his or her best. Here, "strict discipline" is a tactical response to achieve the inner intention of developing the child into a great adult.

But a person may use "kindness" tactically to achieve their inner purpose of luring someone to trap him with a pleasant and smiling demeanor. The exterior smile is a facade and a tactical approach to achieve the inner design of punishing the person.

When we understand the two "tactical" sefirot, namely Netzach and Hod, our perspective of the world changes. We do not look at anything happening around us at face value. We tend to dig deeper to try and see how each event or act works as an "external means to the internal end."

Questions such as "Why do good people suffer?" and "Why are wicked people prosperous?" can be answered by understanding the attributes of the two tactical sefirot. For example, when you see a righteous person suffering in this world, then you need to dig deeper and try to identify the true intent behind God allowing such people to suffer. Perhaps, it is a divine test to increase future payoffs, or it could be a way to cleansing their last few sins so that they are perfect and pure for the future. In the same way, we must delve deep to understand why wicked people appear to prosper. It could be the divine intention to make such people lose themselves in their outward prosperity, which leads to a sense of complacency, thereby forestalling their repentance.

Consequently, their entire reward is used up in their time on earth, leaving nothing for them in the future except total annihilation. There could be many other possibilities too. The important thing to remember is that God's activities and intentions go deep, and what we see are only surface-level events.

Netzach refers to God's Chesed actions. They are inherently kind and compassionate acts. However, they use the pretense of harshness and suffering. Hod, on the other hand, refers to those experiences where the wicked seem to prosper. This is Gevurah in action but through the facade of pleasantness.

The two sefirot, Netzach and Hod, are a turning point in the chain of development of the ten sefirot because these are focused on humans. It is about what is the most appropriate way for humans to be rewarded and punished? What is the best way for humans to receive God's message? How can God's will be effectively implemented?

Another interesting element to think about when talking about Netzach and Hod are the parts of the physical body of God they represent. Netzach represents God's right foot, and Hod represents His left foot. Kabbalists believe that feet are a vital aspect of a person's activity. Hands are the primary instruments of action, while feet are the organs that help individuals with mobility. The feet are the organ that takes a person from place to place so the hands can do the actions.

Another reason God's feet are the symbol of Netzach and Hod is there is little distinction between right and left foot compared to the distinction between right and left hand. Similarly, Chesed and Gevurah are distinctly different (represented by God's hands), while the differences between Netzach and Hod are not far less distinct. Both Hod and Netzach combine Chesed and Gevurah, blurring their distinction.

Interestingly, this blur between Netzach and Hod is one of the primary reasons we find it difficult to discover the true intent and motive for God's actions. Let us take an example to understand how these two "tactical" sefirot enhance our difficulty in understanding God's deep and pure intent.

Suppose you got a huge bonus this year. If you measured this aspect using only Gevurah/Chesed elements, you could tell yourself this is a reward for your good deeds, but now we have to account for Hod and Netzach sefirot too. So, if you take Hod into account, you should ask yourself, "Is this bonus really a reward? Or is it a facade to make me feel good about myself so that I forget to look at my mistakes? Is it a little good for me while a bigger and fuller punishment is waiting to happen?"

So, what is the deeper purpose of the two sefirot? It is not to complicate or confuse us. It is the accentuation of the Divine truth. When you see the attribute of Netzach, and later on you see how the righteous get rewarded, only then can you see how deserved the righteous people are.

By nature, humans are quite sloppy, and we continuously make minor errors. However, these minor errors are usually forgiven, provided the person is generally good, but the benefits received are not earned. However, through the Netzach, which is God's retribution for the faults of the righteous, your ability to sense every bit of goodness you receive far more sharply than without the Netzach.

For Hod sefirot, too, this holds good. When you see the punishment of wicked people, and you see it in the perspective of the good they received, it does not appear as an act of cruel vengeance. Instead, you can see it as deserved retribution.

Netzach stands for conquering or vanquishing. However, it is only an overt act of conquest and seems to be the outcome of Gevurah or strength. Gevurah represents the potential to win, while Netzach is the actual conquest. Hod goes deeper than this idea. Let us take an illustration to understand Hod sefirah a little bit.

When you see an open threat or danger, you feel free, a common human emotion. For example, when someone points a gun or knife at you, then the primary emotion is fear. However, when you see the outcome of hidden power, then it is not fear as much as awe, even if the outcome is of a terrible kind.

For example, when you see a charismatic, powerful leader, you are in awe. He or she may not be carrying a gun. But you feel the imminent strength of this individual. This is the reason many of us get carried away by dictators. At least for a little while, these people seem to have imminent power to sway the innocent toward their way of thinking. On the other side, if you see and interact with spiritually powerful people, you can feel the power of their spiritual strength, and you are in awe even though outwardly, such people are the epitome of modesty and humility.

With God, this imminent power you feel is limitless. And this imminent power is missed by wicked people when they get carried away by the small leeway He gives them before He unleashes the storm they truly deserve.

Yesod or Foundation

The ninth sefirah, Yesod, appears in the middle of the Tree of Life. It has two primary functions, namely:

- To balance out Hod and Netzach.
- To channelize energy from the upper sefirot to the last and tenth sefirah.

Yesod translates to "foundation." It is connected with God's circumcised penis and unites Tiferet with Shekhinah, the last sefirah. Yesod is connected with the biblical character, Joseph, Jacob's son. Joseph was sold off as a slave by his brothers. He landed in Egypt and interpreted the Pharaoh's dreams, and became prosperous and powerful.

The Yesod is called the foundation because it anchors the human world to its spiritual bedrock. You could build the most beautiful house filled with all the conveniences and luxuries. You could have used the most advanced construction techniques to build your house.

But, if your foundation is weak, your house will fall down. The most important functional aspect of a home is its foundation because the entire house is anchored to it. If the bedrock is weak, then the most beautiful house has no value. The universe created by God is like your house, and He made sure this beautiful house rests on solid bedrock.

A Kabbalah saying goes as follows, "God hangs the world on nothingness." The concept of nothingness is not only a reference to a vacuum of space but more so on the purpose of existence. The nothingness refers to the ultimate cause of our existence, which can never be traced. We cannot find the cause of the original cause because that is causeless. This paradox is answered through the attribute of Yesod. This sefirah is the pillar on which the cosmos rests.

This divine pillar is a reference to the divine will that is bestowed on all of us. Absent this divine will, this universe that senses and experiences independence would not exist. It is only because God wanted to bestow the divine will that He created a universe with its own self-contained laws, rules, and regulations. He created the universe in which we perceive ourselves as independent beings only because of His divine will.

It is this divine will that is the pillar extending from the bedrock of reality or God Himself. This pillar is the foundation on which our world is created. Let us use an analogy of a parent's desire to have a child to understand this concept a little better.

A single cell develops into a human through conception. The conception of a child requires two cells, namely that of the mother and the father. However, the action of childbirth starts with the desire of the father. So, the source of that single cell that will form into the human is the father's desire. But if you asked why the father wanted the child, then there is no answer other than the child's existence.

The same argument is valid for the Yesod sefirah. So, the answer to the question, "Why does our world exist?" is, "Because God desired it and wanted to bestow existence on us." And this can be easily understood because the world was created, and we exist in it. Why God wanted to create the world and bestow His blessings is outside the purview of human existence.

God's desire to create is the first interactive contact of humans with God. The answer to "Why He desired?" belongs to the history before humans came into existence. Yesod is the connection or bridge between God and humankind.

The idea of Yesod sefirah also fits into another area in the creation process. The seven days of creation correspond to the seven lower sefirot starting from Chesed until Malchut. Therefore, the sixth day or Friday is related to Yesod. Friday and the Yesod sefirah are connected in two ways:

First, Friday is the day to prepare for Saturday, the Sabbath. The first six days are working days when we work hard and make food, including for Sabbath. On Friday, food preparation from weekdays to Sabbath begins. Also, dessert for Sabbath is prepared on Friday, a concept that symbolizes the double portion of manna (one extra for Sabbath) that fell from the heavens on Friday when the Israelites were in the desert. These events and elements symbolize the idea that Friday was the funnel into Sabbath. Therefore. Friday is the pillar of support for the Sabbath and the workdays and is a foundation, like a sefirah Yesod.

Second, Friday is the day when God created humans. Yesod, as already explained, is the bridge that connects earth with heaven allowing for spirituality and divinity to pass into the material world. Now, there are three beings in our world, namely:

- Plants, animals, and minerals in the materials world - these beings cannot transfer spirituality within themselves because these beings have only a physical form.

- Angels and other such beings in the spiritual world - these beings cannot translate their values into the physical world because they do not have a physical body.

- humans form the third kind of species with a soul and a body. The soul is spiritual, and the body is physical, which together allows for the transition of values from one world to another. Therefore, humans created on Friday are fitting examples of Yesod sefirah.

Summarily, Friday funnels the produce of the other workdays into Sabbath, and humans created on Friday have the power to gather the spiritual produce from the higher planes to shape the world we live in. These two points render Friday, the sixth day of creation, the embodiment of Yesod.

Shekhinah, Malchut, or Immanence

Shekhinah, also called Malchut, translates to "kingdom," which represents the presence of God in the everyday world of humans. It is at the bottom of the Tree of Life and takes all the energies from the previous sefirot and passes this energy on to the human world. It represents God's feet or spine because Shekhinah serves as a foundation of the Tree of Life.

Shekhinah acts as a bridge between our material world and God's realm. It is the only sefirah that actually comes down into the world of humans. The primary goal of all Kabbalists is to create a union between Shekhinah and Tiferet. Shekhinah is God's feminine representative in the human world, while Tiferet is God's masculine side.

According to Kabbalistic belief, when believers perform a righteous action, then Yesod (God's circumcised penis) is stimulated and hastens the union of Tiferet and Shekhinah. In Kabbalah, sexual intercourse and marriages are symbolic of the divine union of Tiferet and Shekhinah. Shekhinah is associated with David, the biblical character who was the second king of the twelve Israeli tribes.

The last and final sefirah is considered the most important of all the ten sefirot. To understand why we must begin by understanding the definition of Malchut or kingdom. What comes to mind when we think of a kingdom? It is usually the image of a dictator who is imposing his will on his helpless subjects to achieve his own personal interests. Even if the ruler was a benevolent one, he is not more than an efficient politician.

In Kabbalah, the "kingdom" defined in the ten sefirot is different. God and His kingdom are of a different model. The king, our God, is one who knows the difference between good and bad and knows right and wrong ideologies. He teaches His subjects values and principles that help them awaken their inner spirit. His subjects then go about building institutions and their society according to God's taught ideologies and principles.

When society is ready, it enhances the values that God, our King, had in His heart and mind. Therefore, in this model, a society built on divine values is not merely expressing the king's principles but also demonstrates these principles are the inner values and norms of the people within that society. This model differs from the traditional kingdom ruled by an autocrat or dictator.

Another good analogy to understand the sefirah of Malchut is the example of a good teacher. A good teacher does not allow his students to do as they please because the teacher has not imparted or given anything to the students. On the other extreme, a teacher who forces his students to do exactly as per his instructions, imposing external barriers and shackles, will not be a good teacher either.

A good teacher inspires students to help them realize their own values and feelings are the same as their teacher has taught them. This state is the same as the tenth sefirah, Malchut. We express God's attributes and actions because He has made us realize that His values are our own inner values. His teachings strike a resonant chord in our hearts, and our actions reflect His teachings.

In His kingdom, we do God's will, but we do so with free will. When we fail to implement God's will, then we do not reflect the Divine process. If we do God's will out of fear, then we are like the uninspired students of that strict, imposing teacher mentioned in the example above.

A key element to remember about Malchut is that it is an attribute that does not emanate directly from the Divine. It emanates from His creation when the creation reflects His glory from itself. There is a large gap between the first nine sefirot and the last one. The first nine continuously emanate as and from God's actions, which affect the human world. When we imbibe these influences of God, find our identity in His values and principles, and reflect His glory, then Malchut is evinced.

In this sefirah, God acts through us and not only by Himself. Malchut was the ultimate goal of Creation, and the other nine sefirot are only the means to achieve this final Divine goal. When it comes to the first nine sefirot, humans are only outside observers. We admire and are in awe of His work and creation. And yet, it is not really an overwhelming experience.

It is only when we experience the voice of God from within us that we truly experience the divine, and that is Malchut. Only then are we transformed.

Analysis of the Ten Sefirot

The first three sefirot, namely Keter, Hokhmah, and Binah, together represent God's head. The combination of these three sefirot is so powerful that seven more sefirot are created after them. The union of Keter, Hokhmah, and Binah results in such powerful energy, it has the force to harness its own energy and channelize it for the process of creation.

The evolution and need for both masculine and feminine energies (as represented by the first three sefirot, which originated from God) to create the world represents that God's infinite power consists of both male and female aspects. Hokhmah is pure intellect and, without Binah (thoughts and ideas), is bereft of direction. Therefore, Kabbalah is deeply rooted in this belief, and both men and women are needed to sustain this world together.

Another interesting aspect of these three sefirot is that the roots of the Tree of Life are not at the bottom but the top. The sefirot evolve from Keter, which connects the infinite power of God to the Tree of Life, and this energy gets channelized into the finite human world. God's infinite energy moves through the Tree of Life from the first sefirah, Keter, down to the last and tenth sefirah, Shekhinah.

So, while the trees in the finite human world draw their energy from the bottom, the energy in the Tree of Life comes from the top, which is connected directly to the Infinite light of God, which pervades the cosmos. God's energy moves downward to our finite world. The human energy must move upward, in the opposite direction, to ultimately merge with God's light.

In the human world, we must start with the tenth sefirah, the Shekhinah, who is God's representative in the material world. Then, we move upwards, getting increasingly closer to Keter and God's infinite light as we learn and grow spiritually.

One of the most controversial thoughts in Kabbalah is the idea that evil stems naturally from God's creative process. It is easy to understand the controversy considering that most religions look at evil as part of humans and that God has no part in it. Evil is most often taken as a "blame" or mistake committed by humans.

However, it is vital to know that in Kabbalah, there is no concept of "blaming" God for evil. Instead, Kabbalists view evil as a necessary element of the cosmos that needs to be kept in check by the sefirot.

Another interesting aspect of the three middle sefirot, namely Hesed, Gevurah, and Tiferet, is their connection to a biblical character. Just as the sefirot follow a specific order in which they were formed, their association with biblical characters also follows a chain.

Chesed is connected with Abraham, whose son was Isaac, who is associated with Gevurah, the sefirah that emerges from Chesed. Tiferet emerges from Chesed and Gevurah, and this sefirah is associated with Jacob, the son of Isaac. The movement of association of the sefirot from father to son represents the idea that each sefirah is a product of its previous one. Like the relationship between parents and children, each sefirah arises from its previous one and impacts the one coming after it.

When you analyze the last four sefirot, one particularly important aspect of Kabbalah comes forth. As compared to many religions that considered talking and discussing the sexual act as taboo, Kabbalah embraces it and even makes it the source for the achievement of the believer's highest aim.

Kabbalists' purpose is to achieve union between Shekhinah and Tiferet, which is important to restore God to a state of wholeness. This feat is not at all easy at, and the tenth sefirah bears most of the burden during this journey. As Shekhinah is the only sefirah in the human world, she is in exile and is stuck in the material world, much against her wishes. The plight of Shekhinah is comparable to the state of Israelites who are exiled from their holy land.

Kabbalists, therefore, believe that doing good deeds can bring the male and female aspects of God together and create a sacred union. This union achieves three important goals simultaneously:

- God is restored to His state of wholeness.
- Shekhinah is freed from exile.
- Israelites return to their holy land.

The sexual act is spoken openly in Kabbalah as it represents the longing of Tiferet to unite with Shekhinah. This longing is explicitly described in many texts as a sexual desire. The feelings of lust between Tiferet and Shekhinah for each other are believed to stimulate God's penis, which helps to reach sexual bliss.

For Kabbalists, the way to stimulate God's penis is by studying Kabbalah and performing good deeds. Another way is to get married and indulge in religiously approved sexual acts. Since ancient times, Friday night, which is the start of the Sabbath, is believed to be Shekinah's holy hour, and therefore, is the best time for sex and marriages.

Chapter Eight: Kabbalah on Good, Evil, Prayer, Punishment, and Souls

Kabbalah's outlook on the subjects of good, evil, prayer, punishment, and soul are all founded on the will of God, the ten sefirot, and His word. Let us look a little deeper into these subjects.

Good and Evil

In Kabbalah, the existence of evil is an important point for discussion. Some Kabbalists believe that evil by itself is not real. When we cannot identify and receive the influx from all the ten sefirot, then evil emanates. Evil results from being estranged from the source of the ten emanations.

Some other Kabbalists believe that evil is the sefirah of power. From this belief emerges a corollary belief that evil and death must also be positive in some ways. These believers argue against the idea that evil is caused when estranged from the influx of the sefirot.

Based on the above ideas, most Kabbalists believe that evil is "Sitra Ahra" or from the other side, as opposed to divinity and God's grace and abundance. "Sitra Ahra" is perceived as counter-sefirot, a place of unclean and dark power versus holiness and goodness of divine power.

Zohar defines evil as follows, "When the night begins, all the powers of evil including evil spirits emerge and roam around the world, and the power of the "other side" is let loose. When this happens, humans experience sensations of death in the middle of their sleep. Three sets of angels separating themselves from their Lord, then descend from heaven and keep watch over our world and, while doing so, sing praises of God. These angels remain separated from God until the "other side" departs from the world."

According to Zohar, the evil forces are continuously engaged in battles with the powers of goodness and holiness. These evil powers were created when Gevurah or Din, the sefirah of judgment, developed abundantly after emerging from Chesed or Mercy, the previous sefirah. The growth of Gevurah became increasingly strong through human sin.

The story of Adam eating the fruit of the Tree of Knowledge is believed to be the first appearance of evil. Eating the fruit is interpreted as separating the fruit from the Tree of Knowledge, activating the potential of evil contained in the tree. The plucking and eating of the fruit are interpreted as a division in the divine unity.

This division causes the channels connecting the upper and lower worlds to become unsettled. The lowest sefirah, Malkhut, was separated from the other nine with Adam's act of eating the fruit from the Tree of Knowledge. The unity between creation and the Creator was broken, resulting in the growth of evil.

Other sins of humans enhance the disturbance in divine unity. Right through in the Torah, these breakages from the divine caused by human sins were repaired only through the good deeds of the faithful heroes. Here is another extract from Zohar that describes evil:

"The pleasures that men indulge in when they sleep give birth to numerous demons. God needed to create all the things in the world to ensure its sustenance and permanence. For example, when He created the brain, He needed to create many layers of membranes around it. In this way, the entire world is made up of various layers starting from the first point of mysticism (with no evil) right up to the farthest point, each layer getting increasingly separated from the starting point. Each of these layers forms q coverings one over another, just like a brain within a brain, a spirit within the spirit, and so forth. Each layer is a shell to another."

Taken in this context, evil is believed to be a "waste product of all the organic processes in the world." Evil can be compared to the dirty water, bad blood, dross obtained when gold is refined, or the dregs of wine. However, Zohar explains that despite everything, there is holiness even on the "other side," regardless of how the evil is believed to be formed. According to Zohar, good and evil are intermingled, and it is our duty to separate them.

The Zohar uses the following parable to explain evil inclination in the cosmos. Why did God create evil? A parable in the Zohar throws some light on this topic. Once, there was a king who had only one son. The king loved his son dearly. He warned his son not to be enticed by prostitutes because they were bad women. Anyone who is defiled by such women would not be allowed entry into his palace.

The son promised his father he would obey this rule out of love for his father. Just outside the palace, a beautiful prostitute had her residence. The king had an idea to test his son's evil inclination. He wanted to see how deeply devoted his son was to him. So, he went to the prostitute and ordered her to entice his son, telling her he wanted to test his son's level of obedience.

The prostitute used every trick she knew to lure the boy into her embrace, but the good son stayed firm and obedient to his father's will. He pushed the prostitute away, and none of her allure worked on him. When the father saw this, he was overjoyed at the obedience his son demonstrated.

So, the king showered him with all the gifts and treasures from the royal treasury, showered praises on him, and honored him too. Now, the Zohar asks, "Who gave the son so much of treasure, praise, and honor?" The cause of this joy and honor was the prostitute. If you look at the entire event in this way, the question that comes to mind is, "Should the prostitute be praised or blamed?"

Zohar says that the prostitute should undoubtedly be praised for two primary reasons. First, she followed her king's orders, obeyed him, and fulfilled his wishes. Second, she caused the son to receive honor and praise and deepened the father-son love.

The lesson from this parable is that evil inclination is necessary to prove one's love and worth. God did lay obstacles on the path of His believers so they could fight against and subdue the evil inclination and demonstrate their love for God. Just as the evil inclination in the prostitute helped illustrate the son's love and commitment to his father's word, the evilness created by God helps us strengthen our love and devotion for Him.

Prayer

In Kabbalah, prayer is a vital part of life because when we pray, we not only acknowledge the existence of God, our Creator, but we also demonstrate our preparedness to follow His will. Prayers help us do the following:

- Praise our God, the Creator.
- Bless His name and Creation.
- Address our needs and requests to Him.
- Ask for forgiveness for our sins.

When we pray, we do so, hoping to receive a favorable response from Him. For this to happen, our prayers must be heard. Here, the concept of "hearing" does not have the same connotation as in the material world. "To be heard by God" means our prayers should be received in the realm of the first three sefirot, namely Keter, Binah, and Hokhmah.

Prayer is also a form of information, and if the information has to reach those high realms, then you must have a clear, unblocked information channel along with sufficient signal strength. Every human in this world is automatically and inherently channeled to God.

However, there are some excellent ways to increase the signal strength and to reduce any blockages:

- By studying the Torah.
- Following the laws contained in the Torah.
- Performing good deeds.
- Reciting blessings.

"Brakhah" is the Hebrew word for blessing. It has the same etymological root as "breikha," which translates to "water channel." Therefore, blessings before a prayer initiate the channel with God, and the signal strength is proportionate to the concentration and sincerity of the prayer.

Kabbalists believe that prayers start at the Malchut sefirah and enter the Yesod sefirah. Yesod is the bridge that connects divinity with the material world. Yesod is also related to the divine name, El-Hai, which means "Living God." When our prayers are accepted, then they ascend the Tree of Life and reach the Binah sefirah. Then, they enter Hokhnah and from there to Keter. Keter, as you already know, represents Divine will and God's desire.

For your prayers to be answered, God's desire to do so must be stimulated, and to do this, your prayers have to reach the Keter sefirah.

Rewards and Punishment

Rewards and punishments are a central theme in Kabbalah. Kabbalists believe in the idea that humans receive rewards for the good work we do and retribution for sins and transgressions. This idea is the basis of human and divine justice in Kabbalah.

In Kabbalah, there is no concept of punishment. There is only the matter of correction so that we may attain the status of perfection. The idea of reward and punishment goes beyond simple materialistic aspects in Kabbalah, especially in the higher spiritual realms. A reward, in the present level of spiritual awareness (for most of us), is about receiving what we want. What we want reflects the depth of our soul's connection with God.

Kabbalists believe that we must strive to reach a state wherein the reward we want is to do something for God, our Creator. At this stage of soul development, the work we do merits reward. Paradoxically, the work you do at this stage is the reward itself. In the end, virtue is its own reward, and vice is its own retribution. The cause and the effect become one at this stage, and you feel a sense of completeness.

Souls

Kabbalists believe that the body and soul are separate entities and yet are indivisible partners in human life. The body is a gift from God and is to be a tool to do sacred work in this world. It is our duty to protect, care for, and respect our body because it is a sacred gift of God.

Three words refer to the soul in the Torah, namely Neshamah, Nefest, and Ruach. Let us look at these three words to understand the concept of soul in Kabbalah. In Genesis, there is an incident wherein God blows a "breath of life" into the man created from earth and dust. The word used for this breath of life is "Neshamah," and describes the element that animates an inanimate object. This element is not distinct from the body and has no personality of its own.

"Ruah" is also used to refer to God's animating force. Ruah's association with the body ends when the mortal body dies. "Nefesh" is the word that refers to the soul with a separate personal dimension. This word is also connected with desire and attraction.

Later on, these three words are used to refer to the soul, which is believed to be a unique, eternal, and intangible part of an individual. When the body dies, the soul returns to God.

Soul and Reincarnation - Reincarnation is a belief that the soul rooted in one body presently could have been living in another body previously. The Hebrew term for reincarnation is "gilgul," which translates to "rolling." Therefore, Kabbalists who embrace the concept of reincarnation believe that the soul "rolls" from one body to another through time.

The Zohar refers to reincarnation in multiple passages. Kabbalists believe that acceptance of this concept is critical to unraveling the mysteries of and understanding several cryptic passages in the Torah. Transmigration of souls to atone for sins is another common point of discussion in the Zohar.

For example, the soul of an excessively proud man is reborn into the body of a worm or bee until the sins are atoned. Similarly, heroes are reborn as other heroes. A passage in Genesis talks about the soul of Cain and Abel's soul entering Moses' body. So, when Jethro and Moses befriended each other, the estrangement between Cain and Abel was rectified.

Judaism discusses three kinds of reincarnation including:

• **Ibbur** - this type is called "impregnation," wherein a soul comes down from heaven to assist another soul in the body.

• **Gilgul** - this is proper transmigration of the soul. Here, the soul that occupied a different body previously is sent back to earth to occupy a new body.

- **Dybbuk** - this type of soul transmigration is a new concept in Judaism. Here, a tortured soul filled with guilt and chased by demons finds rest in a human body. Such souls have to be exorcised.

Now, the concept of transmigration of soul resulted in a philosophical difficulty. The question arises as to what identity can be given to a reincarnated or transmigrated soul because Kabbalist's doctrines are rooted in the idea that body experiences decide the soul's character. Based on this postulate, how can we define a soul that has occupied more than one body?

Zohar counters this argument with a postulate of the existence of the "tzelem" or image. The "tzelem" is described as an astral body that does not transmigrate, thereby maintaining its individual identity. It is vital to remember that when we discuss ideas like transmigration, we are in the space of the occult, and most things in this realm are beyond the limited understanding of the human mind.

This approach is best suited for Kabbalists who know, believe, and accept there are numerous facets in this cosmos that still need to be unraveled and understood before we can reach Ein Sof.

Conclusion

One of the most fundamental beliefs of Kabbalah reflected in the Zohar is that God is unknowable and cannot be described fully using limiting human words. That is why the Almighty is called "Ein Sof" or the Infinite in the Zohar. Learning and understanding the limitless divinity in the Zohar is like trying to create a manmade computer that works like the human brain. The comparison is possible, but a machine can never reach the sophistication of the human brain because the brain was created by God's hands.

The Zohar is a special force with the power to take students and readers to absolute bliss. It is so mesmerizing and thrilling that returning to it multiple times is a common outcome for most students and readers. It is a powerful source of energy and vitality. When you use its powers in your daily life, you can rest assured that you can begin living your life with the power to harness all the good things available on offer.

One of the best things about the Zohar is that anyone can read it and harness its benefits. You need no special skills to understand what is being taught. You need not convert to any new religion to understand the deep purport of life hidden within the depths of the Zohar.

This book is an attempt to get you interested in the vast, unending beauty in the Zohar. The more you read and understand, the more you will realize the power of its ultimate truth. So, go on, read this book again, and when you are ready, delve deeper into the wondrous world of the Zohar.

Here's another book by Mari Silva that you might like

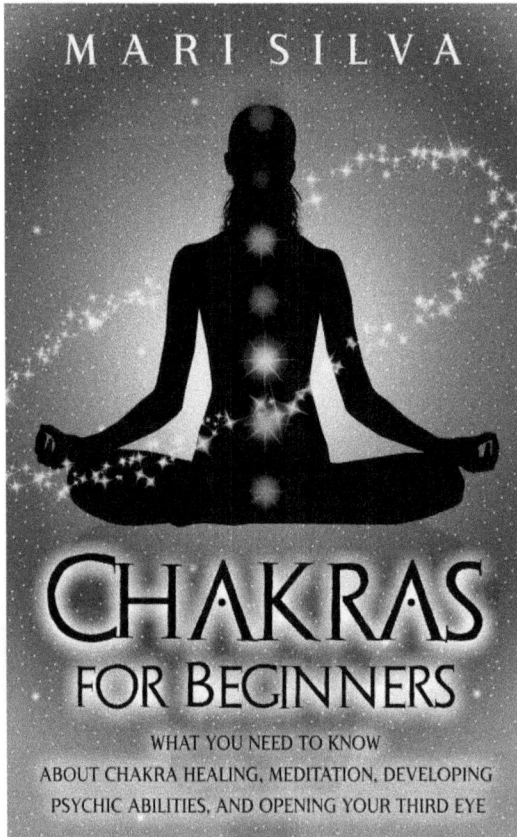

MARI SILVA

CHAKRAS FOR BEGINNERS

WHAT YOU NEED TO KNOW
ABOUT CHAKRA HEALING, MEDITATION, DEVELOPING
PSYCHIC ABILITIES, AND OPENING YOUR THIRD EYE

Your Free Gift (only available for a limited time)

Thanks for getting this book! If you want to learn more about various spirituality topics, then join Mari Silva's community and get a free guided meditation MP3 for awakening your third eye. This guided meditation mp3 is designed to open and strengthen ones third eye so you can experience a higher state of consciousness. Simply visit the link below the image to get started.

https://spiritualityspot.com/meditation

References

Book of Radiance. (n.d.). Www.lapl.org. Retrieved from https://www.lapl.org/collections-resources/blogs/lapl/book-radiance

Chabad.org. (2019). @Chabad.

Cooper-Rosenberg, N. (n.d.). 11 Things You Didn't Know About The Hebrew Language. Culture Trip. Retrieved from https://theculturetrip.com/middle-east/israel/articles/11-things-you-didnt-know-about-the-hebrew-language/

Green, A. (2017, August 25). Restoring Kabbalah to Mainstream Judaism. The Atlantic. https://www.theatlantic.com/international/archive/2017/08/zohar-kabbalah-mainstream-judaism/537621/

INTRODUCTION TO KABBALAH -The Sefirot and the Four Worlds The Sefirot: The Ten Fundamental Essences of Kabbalah. (n.d.). https://resources.finalsite.net/images/v1600236318/wbtlaorg/e04nsdkt ywbb39l6guri/Kabbalah-the-Sefirot-and-the-Four-Worlds.pdf

Kabbalah on how a prayer can change the world. (n.d.). The Jerusalem Post | JPost.com. Retrieved from https://www.jpost.com/kabbalah/a-prayer-that-changed-the-world-634186

Press, S. U. (n.d.). The Zohar: Pritzker Edition, Volume Five | Translation and Commentary by Daniel C. Matt. Www.sup.org. Retrieved from https://www.sup.org/books/title/?id=17671

Sefer ha-zohar | Jewish literature. (n.d.). Encyclopedia Britannica. Retrieved from https://www.britannica.com/topic/Sefer-ha-zohar

Sefirot | Sefaria. (n.d.). Www.sefaria.org. https://www.sefaria.org/sheets/158035?lang=bi

Silber, J. (n.d.). Zohar translation revives poetry and nuance of Jewish mystical text. Www.kalw.org. Retrieved from https://www.kalw.org/post/zohar-translation-revives-poetry-and-nuance-jewish-mystical-text#stream/0

SparkNotes: Today's Most Popular Study Guides. (2019). Sparknotes.com. https://www.sparknotes.com/

The Essential Zohar: The Source of Kabbalistic Wisdom - Kindle edition by Berg, Rav P.S.. Religion & Spirituality Kindle eBooks @ Amazon.com. (2021). Amazon.com. https://www.amazon.com/Essential-Zohar-Rav-P-S-Berg-ebook/dp/B003EY7IFE

The Jewish Website - aish.com. (n.d.). Aishcom. https://www.aish.com/

The power of language in Jewish Kabbalah and magic: how to do (and undo) things with words. (n.d.). The British Library. Retrieved from https://www.bl.uk/hebrew-manuscripts/articles/the-power-of-language-in-jewish-kabbalah#

The Story of Creation according to Kabbalah | InterNations. (n.d.). Www.internations.org. Retrieved from https://www.internations.org/world-forum/the-story-of-creation-according-to-kabbalah-169418

The Zohar. (n.d.). Www.jewishvirtuallibrary.org. https://www.jewishvirtuallibrary.org/the-zohar

V, M. (2019, June 22). My Jewish Learning. My Jewish Learning. https://www.myjewishlearning.com

What is Punishment? | Chapter 11. Concepts in Kabbalah | The Kabbalah Experience | Books | Michael Laitman | Kabbalah Library - Bnei Baruch Kabbalah Education & Research Institute. (n.d.). Www.kabbalah.info. Retrieved from

http://www.kabbalah.info/eng/content/view/frame/85816?/eng/content/view/full/85816&main

Why did God create evil? A Parable from the Zohar – Rabbi Michael Leo Samuel. (n.d.). Www.rabbimichaelsamuel.com. Retrieved from https://www.rabbimichaelsamuel.com/why-did-god-create-evil-a-parable-from-the-zohar/

Zohar: Annotated & Explained (SkyLight Illuminations) - Kindle edition by Daniel Chanan Matt, Harvey, Andrew, Matt, Daniel C.. Religion & Spirituality Kindle eBooks @ Amazon.com. (2021). Amazon.com. https://www.amazon.com/Zohar-Annotated-Explained-SkyLight-Illuminations-ebook/dp/B01HT6DWF2

Zohar: The Book of Splendor: Basic Readings from the Kabbalah: Scholem, Gershom: 9780805210347: Amazon.com: Books. (2021). Amazon.com. https://www.amazon.com/Zohar-Splendor-Basic-Readings-Kabbalah